The Neuro-psychopathology of Written Language

The Neuro-psychopathology of Written Language

Joseph H. Rosenthal, M.D.

Nelson-Hall
nh Chicago

Library of Conress Cataloging in Publication Data

Rosenthal, Joseph H
    The neuropsychopathology of written language

    Bibliography: p. 143
    Includes index.
    1. Reading disability. 2. Agraphia. 3. Neuro-
psychology. 4. Language and languages. I. Title.
RC394.W6R67   616.8'553   77-2825
ISBN 0-88229-382-6

Manufactured in the United States of America

to the parents . . .
that most oppressed majority . . .
may this book in some way . . .
relieve some . . .
of their undeserved feelings of guilt.

Contents

Reading dynamics (success); contradictory evidence /
The psycholinguistic interpretation of the writing-
reading process: the psychological reality of
phonological differences; transformational rules apply
to writing-reading as well as to spoken language /
Piagetian cognitive development and its relation to
writing-reading; egocentricity interferes with learning
to read the words and comprehend the thoughts of
others / Subareas in language functioning: reading
readiness tests; the ITPA, pros and cons

Predicting reading failure—ten tests which form the
basis for a successful predictive index for reading
failure; studies of reading problems in prematures /
Reading incompetence / Secondary reading
incompetency / Primary developmental dyslexia:
definition; still largely a diagnosis of exclusion;
diagnostic overlap with other components of the
minimal brain dysfunctions / Historical methods of
attempting to teach writing-reading: phonics
methods, whole-word methods, kinesthetic methods /
Acquired language disorders: relation between alexia
and aphasia; alexia and dyslexia / Primary
developmental (constitutional) dyslexia or acquired dyslexia
(alexia)? possible overlapping of categories, for example,
congenital arteriovenous anomaly / Perinatal distress
factors in secondary reading incompetence; the
biological continuum of "reproductive casualty"?/
Congenital word blindness and strephosymbolia /
Geographic distribution of developmental dyslexia;
Kana/Kanji differences / Differences between left and
right parietal dysgraphia and dyslexia (alexia) / Genetic
aspects of dyslexia / Sex-linked differences in
cerebral processing

Johnson and Myklebust's categories: auditory and
visual dyslexics / Kinsbourne and Warrington's
categories: a language retardation group and a
Gerstmann group / Bateman's categories: visual
learners, auditory learners, children with deficits in
both visual and auditory skills; therapeutic
implications / Boder's subgroups: dysphonetic,
dyseidetic, and mixed; Boder clarified interrelations
among writing, reading, and spelling errors; created
a diagnostic test for dyslexia and its subgroups

eliminating the need for diagnosis by exclusion; therapeutic implications; sex ratios and percentages of patients in each subgroup; genetic aspects

Feelings of frustration, poor self-concept, and aggressive antisocial behavior / Seldom do emotional problems cause learning failures; rather they are effects

Previous EEG studies not specifically diagnostic / Concept of delayed maturation in dyslexia / Subclinical reading epilepsy? / Auditory evoked cortical potentials in children with MBD: visual evoked cortical potentials in a family of dyslexics; relations between neurophysiological measures of delayed maturation and clinically observed immature behavior / In dyslexic children EEG spectral analysis showed greater mean coherences for all activity within the same hemisphere but in normals the coherences tended to be higher between symmetrical regions across the midline / EEG coherence findings in adult dyslexics similar to those of children; Hanley feels that he can distinguish dyslexics from normals by visual inspection of the standard EEG / Recent neurophysiological research

The method of Doman and Delacato: for a wide spectrum of disabilities; concept of neurological organization; patterning techniques; nonreplication of results by others / The optometric visual treatment approach to children with reading problems; optometrists and ophthalmologists often disagree / Dyslexia caused by cerebellar-vestibular dysfunction rather than by cortical dysfunction? Subclinical nystagmus occurs, causing disordered ocular fixation, disordered sequential scanning of letters and words, resulting in letter and word scrambling, that is, dysmetric dyslexia and dyspraxia

Introduction

Marked deviations from normal behaviors are in some instances easier to deal with than subtle ones because where the relation between cause and effect is clear, understanding of the deviation ensues even though its effect on the patient may be overwhelming. In recent years one of the most outstanding examples of the problems that attend subtle deviations from the normal has been the difficulty that is now appreciated in the recognition, diagnosis, and treatment of those children and adults who have learning disabilities, often as a result of minimal brain dysfunctioning. There are controversies with relation to the existence, diagnosis, prognosis, and treatment of learning disabilities as "subtle" problems of cognition, of behavior, or of both. A twelve-year-old patient with right hemiplegia and dysarthria (difficulties with speech production) who has cerebral palsy, with all its attendant psychological problems, may in some ways be easier to work with and to help than a twelve-year-old youngster who looks fine, talks well, does fairly well in mathematics and baseball, yet cannot read, spell, or write beyond the second-grade level. Epithets based on the belief that the child is exhibiting retardation, psychopathology, poor motivation, malingering, or all of these may well have been hurled at the patient, adding loss of self-esteem to the fundamental problem.

There is a continuum of psychobiological development ranging from a probably nonexistent psychological, mental, and physical perfection to several marked deviations from normalcy, which include the mental retardations, the epilepsies, the cerebral palsies, and the states of deafness and blindness. Unfortunately these organically based abnormalities are not mutually exclusive; all combinations of pathologic deviations exist, each with psychological consequences. In the last thirty years there has been increasing recognition of subtle and marked problems of cognition and/or behavior which manifest themselves in one or more of four major symptom complexes. These are not mutually exclusive; they often result in disastrous secondary psychological problems:

1. The syndromes of the dyslexias-dysgraphias (difficulties in expressing thoughts in appropriate graphic form)

2. The syndromes of motor-perceptual dysfunctions

3. The syndromes of distractibility-hyperactivity-decreased attention span

4. The syndromes of the language delays

Many clinicians and investigators have contributed to the accumulating knowledge about the clinically evidenced, functionally expressed learning disabilities, the underlying neuropsychological states for which are, in most cases, conditions of minimal brain dysfunctioning. Goldstein (1942) described soldiers injured in World War I who exhibited a wide range of cognitive and behavioral difficulties secondary to definite trauma to the central nervous system. In view of his observations of differential and varying disorders depending upon the area and magnitude of the lesion, Goldstein suggested that such trauma does not necessarily destroy or diminish all of one's faculties. Strauss and Lehtinen (1947) and Strauss and Kephart (1955) described children with a wide spectrum of learning and behavior problems, and stressed individual differences. They used terms such as "minor brain damage" and "minimal brain injury," indicating that these states may occur and may cause much difficulty at home and in school, even though the *general* intelligence level may be within normal limits, with marked dichotomies in verbal and performance skills. Although these terms have been widely used, they are unfortunate ones because they connote specific brain alterations, whereas such alterations have not been anatomically or pathologically validated. However, recent neurophysiologic advances may not only clarify understanding of these conditions of cognitive and/or behavioral difficulties, but also establish respectability for the often confused and maligned learning disabilities, with respect to which psychologists, educators, and physicians have struggled and argued.

The organicity-versus-environment argument exists for almost any aspect of human behavior (Clements, 1966). As increasing numbers of children and adults are being identified who have learning problems, the dissatisfaction grows among many workers with attribution of these abnormalities to purely psychogenic and interpersonal causes. Clements believed that at least for the time being the term *minimal brain dysfunction* may be considered pragmatic and acceptable. He considered that it refers to children or adults of near-average, average, or above-average general intelligence who have certain learning and/or behavioral disabilities ranging from mild to severe, which are associated with deviations of function of the central nervous system. These deviations may manifest themselves as various combinations of impaired control of attention, impulse, or motor function, or as impairment of perception, conceptualization, memory, or language.

It is the special aim of this book to discuss the neuropsychology and the neuropsychopathology of written language from historical, comparative, developmental, cognitive-perceptual, neuropsychological, genetic, educational-clinical, and neurophysiological vantage points. It is *hoped* that the book will integrate data—at times confusing and contradictory—accumulated from many different disciplines to establish a clearer and more understandable model of writing-reading-spelling processes and dysfunctions thereof.

Language in humans almost certainly began in prehistory as an auditory-vocal channel of communication. Written language (in a sense corresponding with history) was and is an arbitrary superimposition of systems of graphic symbols upon verbal language, thereby releasing language from the previous restrictions of time and place. Thus a major point of this book is that in order to fully comprehend the normal and pathological processes of written language, a basic understanding of language must first be realized, because the speaker-hearer/writer-reader is one. This is especially noted in Piagetian cognitive approaches to the understanding and teaching of writing-reading-spelling, wherein is stressed the need for the child first to possess developmental and conceptual stages of language. Psycholinguistic approaches to written language emphasize the comprehension aspects of language processing via the rules of transformational grammar and the phonological, syntactic, and semantic levels of sentence structure, component elements of which are noted both in verbal and in written language.

Further support for the close relation between written and verbal language comes from data indicating 1) a high incidence of speech and language problems in those children who later have reading problems, and 2) a high incidence of dysfunctions of written language in those patients with aphasia.

Anatomic and physiologic similarities and differences of peripheral and central mechanisms relating to language and communication are compared and contrasted in humans and other primates. The concept that human language possesses biologically based singular and unmatched design features making it distinct from the communication processes of "lower forms" is being challenged by recent successful attempts to teach language to nonhuman primates.

Definitions of language and communication are presented and also questioned. The psycholinguistic development of "normal" language processes involving a "language acquisition device" and language universals in children are described from the viewpoint of hierarchically constructed generative grammars, in which the speaker-hearer/writer-reader takes an *active* part. Neuropsychopathologies interfering with normal language development such as developmental language delays, hearing loss effects, histidinemia (defined on page 25), and somesthesia (defined on page 26) are overviewed. Differences between speech and language are presented.

Language is symbolic behavior, and the symbols of the symbols are written language. Nonverbal systems of language are discussed, noting the relation between linguistic and kinesic units within one's own behavior as well as among others' behavior. Anthropological and historical antecedents of language and the evolutionary development of cerebral hemispheric specializations from both anatomic and physiological viewpoints are discussed.

Written language has developed through pictographic, ideographic, rebus symbolic, syllabic, and alphabetic stages. Dialects and vernaculars exist in both spoken and written language. Elaborate and restricted socio-language codes which may predispose to different behavioral and cognitive styles are described.

The historical conflict between nativist and empiricist conceptual approaches to learning and development is discussed from the points of view of the organic lamp versus the mechanical mirror theorists. Psychoanalytic theories with relation to primary psychogenic causes for writing-reading-spelling problems are described.

There are many models stemming from educational, psychological, and medical disciplines purporting to ex-

plain wholly or in part the normal and abnormal development of writing-reading-spelling processes. Associationistic, psycholinguistic, Piagetian cognitive, and information
processing approaches are compared and contrasted, and
subareas of language functioning as assessed by the Illinois Test of Psycholinguistic Abilities (ITPA) are evaluated. In addition, at the end of the book three 'out-of-
the-mainstream" approaches to written language dysfunction are discussed because the unreplicated data engendered by those approaches point up the very complex and
controversial issues related to interactions among organic
and psychogenic variables in this area. Unfortunately
these issues oftentimes are voiced and judged in the popular press with little heed given to scientific rigor. These
approaches include the Doman-Delacato Patterning
Method, the optometric-visual methods, and the theory
that dyslexia is a cerebellar-vestibular dysfunction.

Writing-reading-spelling is a most complex process,
involving at least visual and auditory perception, discrimination, sequential memory and recall, and directional orientation. It also requires visual-auditory integration, fine
motor and visual-motor coordination, and tactile-kinesthetic memory (Boder, 1971). The end point of the process
of writing-reading-spelling is comprehension, and maturational and motivational factors are constantly inter-
twined with those mentioned. It is little wonder that a
minor dysfunction in any of these complicated and inter-
related processes can cause a deficient final product.

Dysfunctions of writing-reading-spelling processes in
modern life, which is in great part dependent upon successful encoding and decoding of graphic symbols, can be
overwhelming. Therefore predicting reading failure has become an important educational goal and many readiness
programs have been developed to prevent reading incompetence. The various therapeutic approaches to the remediation of reading incompetence, including phonics, sight-
see, tactile-kinesthetic, and combinations thereof, attest

to the complexity and the many-faceted aspects of writing-reading-spelling problems. There is a hard core group of reading incompetents who still seem to have great difficulty in learning to write-read-spell by conventional teaching methods even though they can see and hear, have no gross neurologic deficit or primary emotional disturbance, have a "general IQ" within normal limits, and have no socio-motivational causes for their problem—that is, those with primary developmental dyslexia.

Whether primary developmental dyslexia is due to subtleties of "brain-dysfunction-damage" or whether the etiology is of a genetic nature, or both, is controversial. Perinatal malnutrition seems to play a significant role. Overlapping diagnostic categories offered by proponents of many different disciplines advocating different treatment approaches often add to the already existing hávoc in those patients (and their families) who cannot write-read-spell with no discernible cause. The secondary emotional problems are often severe.

Acquired disorders of language, both written and spoken, are discussed (alexias, aphasias, dyslexias, dysgraphias) because of their clinico-anatomical importance in the establishment of areas of functional localization in the central nervous system (CNS). Added descriptions of braille and Morse code dyslexia-dysgraphia, as well as the studies of "bilingual" Kana-Kanji language disturbances add new data about different CNS styles of processing kinesthetically as well as visually-auditorially, and about processing ideographic as opposed to syllabic scripts.

The differences between the alexias-agraphias due to lesions of the left and right hemispheres as described by Hécaen (1967), Critchley (1970a), and Luria (1973) suggest that at least two types of perceptual-cognitive processes are involved in writing-reading-spelling talents. This is supported by the work of Bateman (1968), Johnson and Myklebust (1967), Kinsbourne and Warrington (1966), and Boder (1968, 1971). Boder suggested that there seem to be at least two subtypes of primary developmental dyslexia in children and adults, dysphonetic (defined on page 113) and dyseidetic (defined on page 114), and stressed appropriate remedial approaches for each type.

The recent neurophysiological studies of Conners (1970), Callaway and Harris (1974), Sklar (1971), and Galin and Ornstein (1973) suggest that one can obtain appropriate and significant neurophysiological measures using cortical evoked potentials, spectral analysis, and coherence and coupling techniques, for ongoing cognitive functioning and for differences obtained when dysfunctions of cognitive processes are present. In addition it appears that preferred cognitive styles (biologically based?) may exist because some persons tend to process information via a left hemisphere-propositional verbal-analytic approach, while others tend to use a right hemisphere-appositional-spatial-relational style. A person's preferred cognitive style may facilitate his learning of one type of subject matter, for example, spatial-relational, while hampering the learning of another, such as verbal-analytic. One's difficulties with writing-reading-spelling when only a phonics (left?) or whole-word-Gestalt (right?) teaching approach is used may arise from his or her inability to change by cognitive flexibility to, or to integrate, the cognitive mode appropriate to the work required. Perhaps Boder's dysphonetic and dyseidetic subgroups are extreme versions, neurophysiologically and genetically based, of these inabilities to alternate or to integrate cognitive styles.

The establishment of the diagnosis of and specific testing for primary developmental dyslexia allows for more individual remediation and realistic prognosis. By making it no longer a diagnosis by exclusion, it has given definition and in a sense respectability to a previously much maligned condition.

Future collaboration among the neuropsychologist, the clinician, and the electrophysiologist might include design of appropriate verbal and spatial tasks for adult (to rule out maturation effects) dysphonetic and dyseidetic dyslexics and, by appropriate neurophysiological studies, elucidation of the CNS substrates for normal and abnormal processes of writing-reading-spelling.

The last fifty years have seen great changes from the times when one who could not write-read-spell without discernible cause was considered to be retarded, psychopathologic, poorly motivated, and/or malingering.

I
Communication and Language

Definitions

In order to discuss the neuropsychology and the neuropsychopathology of written language, it is necessary to define communication and language.

The term *communication* derives from the Latin *communicare*, "to make common, to share, to impart, to transmit." Communication is a process that is purposeful and interactive, in that it passes along information in a meaningful sense. Communication in its broadest interpretation may be defined as an eliciting of a response (Dance, 1967). Hockett (1958) thought of communication as "those acts by which one organism triggers another." Transmissions may occur by, but are not limited to, sound, light, touch, odor, taste, facial and body signs (kinesics), writing oneself a memorandum, radio signals, bee dancing, stickleback courtship, herring gulls' care of their young, gibbon calls (Hymes, 1967), and thermostat functioning. A complete system of communication mediated by pheromones (social hormones occurring in two insect orders, the Hymenoptera—ants, bees, wasps, and the Isoptera— termites) is the basis for social organization necessary for the survival of the species.

1

Five components—source, transmitter, channel, receiver, and destination—comprise the idealized communication system (Miller, 1951). Communication involves a sender who expresses or encodes a message and a receiver who interprets or decodes it. If the receiver's response or reactions to the original messages are made known to the sender feedback occurs, completing the round of interaction.

The term *language* derives from the Latin *lingua*, "tongue." It may be defined as a system of conventional spoken or written symbols by means of which human beings communicate. Since humans live in socially organized groups, they learn to participate in the behavior patterns of their individual cultures. This behavior consists in the interactions among humans as well as between humans and their environments, and often requires the use of language as a communication method. The science of linguistics is the systematic study of language as distinct from the study of languages for the purpose of being able to speak, read, and write them.

In all human languages there are two kinds of building blocks—the *phonemes*, which are the meaningless basic sounds that can be perceived as differing from one another (Gleason, 1961), and the *morphemes*, the meaningful elements in a language such as words and syllables. The morphemes constitute an enormous stock, yet they are created by varied arrangements of the phonemes, a minuscule stock of distinguishable sounds, each having no specific meaning.

Human and animal communication: human language is/is not unique

Animal communication systems manifest those capabilities of information processing and transfer necessary for their preservation and development. An age-old argument persists as to whether or not there is linear phylogeny of biological communication systems. Efforts to document the linear evolution of human language from the communication systems of lower forms have not been highly successful (Chase, 1966). The arguments for nonlinear phylogeny are anatomic, neurophysiological, philosophical, and emotional. A growing concept among psycholinguists is that human language is a species-specific, innate, genetically determined function of being human.

Darwin, who was interested in psychological as well as structural continuity, believed that novelty and continuity are not compatible. He suggested that a feature in evolution such as *human* language could not really be unique, but that a predictor or hint of it could be discovered, if searched for, in lower animal forms.

Hockett's design features of language

Hockett (1960) described thirteen "design features" that characterize language. Is there a unique cluster of some of these which qualitatively defines human language? Von Frisch's (1950) monumental study of bees has caused speculations about the uniqueness of human language. The bee system of communication has been cited as a curious parallel to our own, in view of the existence in both of Hockett's (1960) design features of semanticity, displacement, and productivity.

Displacement. Human utterances can be displaced or not, depending on the requirement that the linguistic message refer to things remote in space, time, or both, from the communication site. Primate calls are never displaced whereas bee dances always are. Displacement makes for retention and foresight.

Productivity. The productivity of human language is open-ended in that a list of all possible human sentences could not be drawn up. The productivity of bee communication, on the contrary, is limited to the formulation of new messages within a genetically fixed collection of domains, that is, quality, direction, and distance of food sources. The call system of the gibbons, which with the great apes are man's closest living relatives, is closed. It

comprises a small, finite repertory of familiar calls and productivity does not exist. The similarities between bee dancing and human language are of an analogous (functional)
rather than of a homologous (structural) nature (Slobin,
1967). Similarly, bees and birds both fly, but they use analogous rather than homologous organs to do so. It seems
that bees and humans have independently evolved ways
of referring to absent objects.

Traditional (or *cultural*) transmission comprises those
detailed and subtle conventions of any language and the
acquiring of one particular language among many possible languages that are transmitted extragenetically by
learning and teaching.

Duality of patterning is illustrated by the English
words, *tack, cat,* and *act.* These words are distinct as to
meaning, yet are composed of just three basic meaningless sounds in different arrangements. Duality of patterning makes for flexibility and efficiency. Perhaps only in
some birds might the design feature of duality of patterning be found, wherein individual notes may be meaningless unless combined into a meaningful whole.

In reviewing the thirteen design features or language
universals discussed by Hockett (1960), it would appear
that those of productivity and displacement, and those
of traditional transmission and duality of patterning can
be regarded as the cluster that is crucial or nuclear to
human language. The communication system of no lower
form possesses all of these four design features.

Functional and anatomic differences between man and other primates

Peripheral, vocal, and articulatory systems. Lenneberg
(1967) called attention to the unique specializations and
distinctive features in human anatomy and physiology of
peripheral and central nervous system structures. He considered that the differences between these structures in
man and in other primates are not simply of degree, but

of kind, as can be seen when one compares the morphology of language-relevant structures of man with those of our closest of kin, the Pongidae (the great apes, chimpanzee, and gorilla). Man is the only primate able to structurally and functionally use tongue, cheeks, and lips together with the teeth as articulating organs. Subhuman primates breathe through the nose even when the mouth is open because the mouth can be closed off by the meeting of the epiglottis and the palate. Articulation as we know it in man could not have become effective until the epiglottis had descended sufficiently to clear the nasopharyngeal space, so as to allow the expiratory air stream through the oral cavity without obstruction. Because man has an especially strong musculature about the lips and cheeks, combined with a relatively small mouth, he can build up intra-oral air pressure and suddenly release it to produce *p's* and *b's*, or he can sustain that pressure to form *m's*. One muscle, the risorius (Santorini's muscle), has no undisputed homologue in any subhuman form. The teeth of man are markedly even in height and width. Noticeably absent are the enlarged canines so manifest in the males of most other primates. These morphological characteristics of man's dental structure are prerequisite to the production of spirant sounds—*f, v, s, sh, th*. Lenneberg adduced as a final argument the observation that adult patients with pathologic oral structural defects such as amputated tip of the tongue, harelip, or cleft palate manage to produce sounds adequately approximating those of normal speech, whereas other primates with normal oral configurations cannot do so. Lenneberg suggested that the subhuman primates' inability to approximate human sound indicates basic neurophysiological as well as morphological differences.

Central nervous system. Specific differences between man and other primates with respect to the anatomy and physiology of the central nervous system are less clearly identifiable than those which relate to the peripheral vocal-articulatory systems. But there are differences. The skull of the gorilla has a capacity of about 500 milliliters, whereas that of modern man varies between 1,000 and 2,000 milliliters. The frontal and temporoparietal lobe cortex in man shows relative increases not seen in lower forms. These increases are not confined to speech and language areas alone; they also involve other areas which relate to general cognition and intelligence, such as memory, planning, and tool use. Human brains are more extensively convoluted than are those of lower forms, and the average cortical thickness has remained constant, allowing the total volume of the cortex to expand. Paralleling the general primate trend up the phylogenetic scale is an increase in histologically differentiated areas in the cerebral cortex.

Interestingly, as the brain expands, distances between cell bodies increase and thus cell density decreases. By this process the length, arborization, and quantity of dendrites increase as do axodendritic synapses. These developments might well account for a *qualitative* distinction between man and lower forms—that of a very functionally *integrated* central nervous system with complex association tracts, both within the cortex and from the cortex to deeper brain areas.

Yet when brain-weight/body-weight ratios of man and selected primates were compared (Lenneberg, 1967), they were found to be remarkably similar. Appreciation of this observation is modified by inherent difficulties in measuring brain-weight/body-weight ratios across species. For example body weights vary more widely than do brain weights. For some animals it is advantageous to carry about large masses of energy-storing tissue, whereas others must travel as lightly burdened as possible. Furthermore over the life spans of various primates there are at times inconsistent relations between comparative chronological and maturational ages. Lenneberg stressed however that man shows a *unique maturational history*. All lower forms approach the adult condition at a faster pace than does man.

("Young adulthood" is defined as that age at which no further growth in the long bones is recorded.)

As interpreted by Lenneberg the developmental history of the brain is seen as species-specific when one notes that man's brain weight at birth is only twenty-four percent of his adult brain weight, whereas the chimpanzee begins life with a brain that is already sixty percent of its final weight. During the first quarter of the normal lifespan, the chimpanzee's brain gains only thirty percent, man's gains sixty percent.

Some clear differences are noted when the motor homunculi of man (Penfield and Rasmussen, 1950) and of monkey (Woolsey and Settlage, 1951) are compared, even though their topographic projections on their respective motor cortices are similar. In the human brain much of the motor cortex is devoted to controlling vocalization and the use of the hands while in the monkey the cortical areas involved in hand and foot control are about equally developed.

In both lower and higher mammals the old cortex occupies a large convolution that surrounds the brain stem —the limbic lobe (MacLean, 1973). The limbic cortex aids the mammal in viewing its environment and learning to survive. The neocortex, which developed late in the evolutionary scheme, is involved in the creation and preservation of ideas and those abstract thoughts needed for reading, writing, and arithmetic. The neocortex receives signals largely from the visual, auditory, and somatic systems and is concerned primarily with the external environment while the limbic system is oriented internally. The former relates more to thinking, the latter to feeling. There are in addition chemical differences between the limbic cortex and the neocortex.

Geschwind (1965) suggested that a unique anatomical structure of the neocortex which has no real analogue or homologue in lower forms enables man to free himself to some extent from the limbic system which, as an association area, involves emotions and mediates instinctive physical, rather than cognitive, responses to hunger, fear, sex, and rage in lower forms. Animals can form associations cross-modally when strong affect is aroused. In monkeys, for example, these communications manifest themselves as cries and gestures of pleasure or pain. Geschwind contended that this evolutionary new structure is the (left) inferior parietal lobule, which includes the angular gyrus (an elevated convolution on the surface of the brain) and supramarginal gyrus and is at the point of juncture of the cortical projection areas for vision, hearing, and somesthesis. This association area for association areas permits the intermodal associations necessary for object naming, a fundamental requirement of language function. To enable man to name objects, some cognitively based cross-modal relation is required between the visual and auditory association areas in the brain; for example, a child easily learns many new words daily by relating such an auditory stimulus as "broom" with the visual stimulus "broom" with the tactile stimulus "broom." Here again, we note the relation between phylogeny and ontogeny—the area of the angular gyrus matures cytoarchitecturally very late, often in late childhood. And not until seventeen months of age does Broca's area attain the degree of histo-anatomical differentiation shown by other motor centers of the cortex some six months before (Sloan, 1967), again suggesting a possible correlation between clinically observed stages of speech and language development and neurophysiologic maturation.

Grammar and naming abilities are separable skills. Lesions in the area of the angular gyrus relate to decreases in naming ability but do not affect grammatic skill. The patient with anomic or amnestic aphasia suffers from fluent aphasia in which both comprehension and repetition are preserved. When the lesion occurs acutely as a result of vascular occlusion, the lesion most commonly lies in the region of the angular gyrus or in the adjacent portion of the lower temporal lobe (Geschwind, 1971). Geschwind went so far as to indicate that the concept of left cerebral dominance in man is related to the parietal areas' ability to make cross-modal connections.

In summary, assessing differences between human and lower primate forms with relation to function and structure of the peripheral vocal articulation apparatus, and the central nervous system, Lenneberg argued that phonematization, concatenation, and grammatization are beyond purposiveness. Language cannot be traced back to an aphonemic, agrammatical, or simple imitative stage. Lenneberg regarded the beginnings of speech and language as species-specific and biologically based, and as characteristically human manifestations of innate behavior patterns, released and influenced by environmental conditions.

Attempts to teach language to nonhuman primates

General considerations. In spite of the seemingly qualitative differences between human and animal communication, psychologists have for many years been intrigued with the possibilities of teaching various animals, especially chimpanzees, to speak and understand human language. The underlying belief of the learning theorists is that the laws of conditioning are not species-specific and that their systematic and assiduous application should therefore enable lower forms to acquire and use human language. Brown (1958) cited the classic story of Herr von Osten's horse, "der kluge Hans," who seemed to be able to code human speech and queries into correctly answering hoofbeats. Belief in Hans' anthropomorphism and humanlike intelligence waned markedly when appropriate testing showed that the entire performance was one of simple instrumental conditioning. Brown stressed that no animal raised by man, however nurtured and tutored, has ever approached participation in human language. Animals' greatest difficulty is in speech production. Birds imitate human speech better than do chimpanzees and some birds have been able to learn to produce a small number of approximations to words in various languages. Mowrer (1950) suggested that some birds have even learned to use words referentially and expressively. But Brown countered that no bird has ever created novel and acceptable combinations of words it knows, for example, the productivity of Hockett's design features. In addition, even though birds seem to do well in the imitation of human speech, there is very little indication that they can understand human commands, an accomplishment easily attained by dogs.

The Kelloggs and Gua. Brown cited the attempt of Professor and Mrs. Kellogg in 1931 to raise a seven-and-one-half-month-old female chimpanzee, Gua, with their son, Donald, then nine-and-one-half months old. For nine months both "infants" were treated like a human child in every way with regard to feeding, attention, language, and diapering. The Kelloggs allowed Gua to learn human language *incidentally* rather than purposively and after nine months Gua was responding distinctively and correctly to about seventy utterances, just a handful fewer than Donald. However Donald had already begun to respond appropriately to new word combinations which he had never heard before, whereas Gua had to use trial and error in responding to new word combinations.

The Hayeses and Viki. In 1947, Keith and Cathy Hayes adopted a female baby chimpanzee, Viki, immediately after birth. They, in contradistinction to the Kelloggs, attempted to teach Viki *purposively*. After three years Viki managed to enunciate three words, "papa," "mamma," and "cup." Many have doubted, however, that Viki's words truly resembled human articulation. Like Gua Viki infrequently responded to novel combinations of familiar and presumably comprehended words.

Language, depending on its definition, may
exist in nonhuman forms

In recent years work with primates other than man
has generated data to support the concept that language, depending upon its definition, may exist in nonhuman forms. Gardner and Gardner (1969), reviewing the
work of the Hayeses with the chimpanzee Viki, agreed
with Lenneberg (1967) that indeed the vocal apparatus of
the chimpanzee is markedly different from that of man. In
addition vocal behavior of the chimpanzee occurs in
situations of high excitement and tends to be specific to
the exciting situation. Therefore, when one thinks of behavior, communication, and language in general, it may
seem almost unfair to superimpose a nonappropriate
medium of communication on this species.

The use of hands, however, is a prominent feature of
chimpanzee behavior and these animals do well when faced
with manipulatory mechanical problems. Chimpanzees
have little difficulty in using human tools because of the
development of certain parallel cognitive faculties in the
brain, but perhaps a major contribution is the well-developed saddle joint in the thumb. Napier (1962) explained that most primate hands are capable of the movements of convergence, divergence, prehension, and opposition. True opposability appears for the first time among
the primates in the Old World monkeys, in which the car-
pometacarpal joint (the joint between the base of the
thumb and the wrist) manifests a well-developed saddle
configuration comparable to that in the corresponding
joint of the human hand. This allows the thumb to rotate
on its longitudinal axis through an angle of about forty-
five degrees. The thumb can thus be swept across the palm,
and its pulp can be directly opposed to the pulp surfaces
of one or all of the other digits.

*The Gardners and Washoe: teaching American Sign
Language.* Gardner and Gardner chose to work with the

chimpanzee because of this animal's marked sociability. In view of the chimpanzee's spontaneous and mimicking gesturing tendencies, Gardner and Gardner, using American Sign Language (ASL, the language used by the deaf in North America), developed a standardized system of gestures that provided a means of two-way communication with a female chimpanzee, Washoe. The ASL can be compared to pictographic writing, in which some symbols are arbitrary, some representational or iconic. Training methods included imitation, instrumental conditioning, and shaping techniques. Washoe was about one year old when the experiment began. After about two years she was able to use spontaneously and appropriately about thirty signs, including simple demands such as "come-gimme," "more," "hear-listen," and "tickle," and noun signs, which she used to name not only actual objects but also pictures of objects such as hat, clothes, flower, shoes, and key. It is noteworthy that Washoe was able to transfer the "dog" sign to the sound of barking by an unseen dog.

Possible relations to levels of Piagetian stages, cognitive development, and psycholinguistic stages of development. These examples of *levels of representation* may have Piagetian analogues, in that representation varies in degree of abstractness and some acts tend to be internalized and operationalized at different times. Piaget describes the child who, while still in the preoperational stage (ages two to seven years), is cognitively at the *index level*. In response to reference-giving clues he would indicate "duck" on seeing duck footprints and "telephone" on hearing the sound of ringing. At the *symbol level* the child is able to deal with the representations of the objects that are distinct from the objects themselves. These representations are not part of or causally related to the real objects, but exist as separate entities, so that the child as he develops cognitively must construct a link between the real object and its representation. Examples range from relatively realistic photographs to relatively abstract line drawings. For Piaget there is one higher level—that of the *sign*, or representation through written words, which develops between the stages of concrete (ages seven to eleven years) and formal (ages eleven upward) operations. This level represents the most abstract means of representation, that is, a completely arbitrary configuration of marks in a peculiar shape and arrangement (Weikart et al., 1971): alphabets and their use in writing-reading-spelling.

For Washoe the signs, once acquired, did not remain specific to the original referents, but were transferred spontaneously to a wide class of appropriate referents. For example Washoe came to see the sign "key" appropriately, but after a while she asked for keys to various locks with which she was presented when no keys were in sight. From the time that Washoe had eight to ten signs in her repertoire she began to use them in strings of two or more. Some of the combined forms may have been imitations, but many were inventions of her own, such as "gimme-tickle" and "open-food-drink" (for the refrigerator), thereby closely paralleling the productivity and innovative combination that are criteria for human language. Washoe had acquired the pronouns "I-me" and "you." When these occurred in combinations Gardner and Gardner believed that they resembled short sentences. Four signs—"please," "come-gimme," "hurry," and "more," used with one or more other signs—accounted for the largest share of Washoe's early combinations. In general Gardner and Gardner indicated that these four signs functioned as *emphasizers*, as in "please-open-hurry" and "gimme-drink-please". Perhaps these are analogues to the "pivots" (Braine, 1963) or "operators" (Miller and Ervin, 1964) which are described in early stages of the development of a child's language, discussed later in this book.

Fouts (1973) taught two male and two female chimpanzees ten signs of the ASL. The four chimpanzees differed in the rates at which they acquired the signs. In addition they found it relatively easy to learn signs such as "listen," "key," "drink," and "shoe," while others, such as "string," "look," and "hat," caused difficulty. This may be because some of the signs were similar to pre-experimental behaviors in the chimpanzees' repertoire while others were not. Or, for example, the sign "look" (touching the finger near the eye) might arouse aversion because of the tendency to protect the eye.

Premack, Sarah, and bits of plastic; Yerkish: a language; innovation and productivity; traditional transmission? Premack (Fleming, 1974) taught his chimpanzee Sarah by using as symbols a set of small pieces of plastic which varied in shape and color. Each piece stood for one word, so that chimpanzee "language" might now remain as permanent. Sarah learned her 130 symbols via standard conditioning techniques. At the end of two-and-one-half years of training Sarah used words, sentences, the interrogative, class concepts, negation, pluralization, conjunction, quantifiers, the conditional, and the copula. At times she would steal the symbols from her teacher, form her own questions, and answer them correctly. Lana, a three-year-old chimpanzee, can operate a typewriter with fifty keys. Each key has a colored background on which are displayed white geometric configurations. The configurations represent words in a special language called Yerkish, named for Robert M. Yerkes, the primatologist. Projectors flash the configurations, which Lana selects on a screen in front of her. Not only can Lana ask for food, drink, and companionship, she can also check her sentence on the screen and erase it if it is not correct.

In assessing the language that chimpanzees have been able to show us by their performance, it would seem that we are not justified in supposing that we have yet arrived at an understanding of their levels of competence. Are these primates functionally capable of possessing those cross-modal connections of the angular gyrus which

Geschwind believes to be uniquely human? Work now in progress with gorillas at Stanford University indicates that the gorillas sign not only *among*, but also *to*, themselves. A gorilla was asked to sign for a new word whose referent was an acacia leaf. The gorilla signed "tree hair" (Galin, 1975). A crucial question is whether primates, once having been taught signing, will sign to and teach signing to their offspring without human interference—the *traditional transmission* of Hockett's design features. The chimpanzees appear to possess within their language capabilities semanticity and productivity, and possibly traditional transmission and displacement. Only duality of patterning seems to remain as a distinctly human feature.

Development of human language

Language acquisition device

Lenneberg (1967) saw the species-specificity and innate capability for language as being uniquely human, almost in the sense of a biologically based organic language acquisition device. Slobin (1966) discussed the concept of such a *language acquisition device* as a "process" rather than a "content." It appears that human infants are born not so much with a set of linguistic categories as with a set of procedures and inference rules which they use to process language data.

Language universals

The term *language universals* refers to those similarities which exist for all natural human languages encountered everywhere. Slobin suggested that language universals are the result of an innate cognitive competence. In a sense language universals are prelinguistic and psychological. Language universals may be classified as grammatical, semantic, or symbolic and phonologic. They have to do, for example, with distinctions between rules of formation and transformation, the distinction between base and surface structure of a sentence, and definitions of various grammatical relations such as subject-predicate and main verb-object (McNeill, 1966a), as explained below.

Grammatical universals. Examples of grammatical universals (Greenberg, 1966) are:

"*Universal 17.* With overwhelmingly more than chance frequency, languages with dominant order—verb-subject-object—have the adjective after the noun."

"*Universal 32.* Whenever the verb agrees with a nominal subject or nominal object in gender, it also agrees in number."

Results of prospective cross-cultural studies appear to indicate that the underlying grammatical relations expressed by early childhood utterances are universal in that all embody such basic notions as agent, action, object, and locative (Slobin, 1971).

Semantic universals. To establish the existence of semantic universals one would have to prove that identical metaphors could be independently created by different peoples with languages which have no historical connections. Ullmann (1963) cited Tagliavini, who compared the names for the "pupil of the eye" in various idioms. The Greeks had noticed that the hole in the center of the iris of the eye was a reducing mirror in which the observer could see himself or herself as an animated marionette. Evidence for this is that the Greeks used the same word, *Kórē*, for "girl," "doll," and the hole in the iris (Gore, 1965). The ophthalmological *Kórē* of Aristotle (*De-partibus animalium*) was rendered by Celsus in Latin as a diminutive of a diminutive, that is, *pupilla*, from *pupula*, from *pupa* (Latin "baby talk" for "doll"). This analogy between a child and a minute figure reflected in the eye is embodied in the words for "pupil" in other Indo-European languages, for example Spanish *niña* (*del ojo*) and Portuguese *menina* (*do ôlho*). But examples of the same concept and presumably the same etymology are found in some twenty non-Indo-European languages as different from one another as Swahili, Lapp, Chinese, and Samoan. The Hebrew word for the ophthalmic pupil is *eshon ayin,* or "little man of the eye." In certain rural areas of Hessia, the current term for pupil of the eye is *Kindchen* (little child) or *Männchen* (little man).

Another example of the concept of semantic universals has to do with the extended uses of sensation vocabulary in human languages. If these are historical accidents—that is, if they occur only in English, for example—rather than universal metaphors, then these extensions should not be found regularly in languages with no historical connection to English. But Asch (1955) found that Old Testament Hebrew, Homeric Greek, Chinese, Thai, Malayan, and Hausa all had morphemes that are used to name both physical and psychological qualities. The pairings were identical with some found in English. These observations suggest that the referents have shared attributes, creating identical metaphors in different peoples.

Some partial differences did exist however. For example, the morpheme for "hot" indicates rage in Hebrew, enthusiasm in Chinese, sexual arousal in Thai, and energy in Hausa. Still there is a relatedness in the range of meanings.

Parallel developments are not restricted to autonomous metaphors. Metonymic associations may be fairly ubiquitous. "Tongue" is used in the sense of language in many Indo-European idioms—English *tongue,* Latin *lingua,* Greek *glossa,* Russian *jazyk.* But the same relationship is also found in Finno-Ugrian, Turkish, and some African languages.

Language development in infants and children

Psycholinguists suggest that infants and children pass through stages of language development much as they pass through Piagetian stages of cognitive development. The relations between language and cognitive maturation may be more than just parallel developments. They may even be interlocked in the sense that a child cannot use a word with understanding unless he first has the concept of the meaning of the word (Brislawn, 1975). The grammar possessed by infants and children at each of these psycholinguistic stages seems to be unique to that specific stage; it is not merely a diminutive form of an adult grammar. Active grammars can be studied when infants start putting together their earliest two-word utterances, usually at about eighteen months of age. These are not just unstructured juxtapositions of two chance words.

Functional classes of words: pivots (operators) and an open class: their universality. Longitudinal distributional analysis reveals two distinct functional classes of words. There is a small class of "pivot words" (Braine, 1963) or "operators" (Miller and Ervin, 1964) and a large open class containing all the other vocabulary units except the pivot words or operators. The pivot-operator group is small, expands slowly, has a relatively fixed position, contains words of high frequency, and is attached to the open class, thereby opening up the child's language productivity. Fairly typical pivot-operators are "allgone," "byebye," "big," "this," "boy," "girl," "more," and "hi" (McNeill, 1966b). Productivity in this stage of child grammar occurs when, for example, the pivot-operators "allgone" and "more" are combined with words of the open class to create often novel utterances such as "boy allgone," "milk allgone," "hot allgone," and "more hot," "more sing," "more high." Even though the child's grammar at this stage has but two classes of words, these classes cut across the established classes of adult language (verbs, nouns, adjectives, etc.). Slobin (1971) indicated that there is evidence, though limited, for the existence of a type of pivot-operator structure in Bulgarian, French, German, Japanese, Luo (Kenya), Russian, Samoan, Serbian, and Finnish, again stressing the universality of the pivot-operator versus the open-class dichotomy.

Hierarchical constructions of a generative grammar;

transformational grammar. In children with "normal" language development, there is chronologic development of hierarchical constructions, that is, subject-predicate constructions, qualitative and quantitative modifications, transformations involving affirmative-negative, declarative-interrogative, and active-passive constructions. Not only is a grammar generative, in that it should be able to predict or produce all possible sentences in a language, but it must also possess transformational qualities (Chomsky, 1965).

Surface (phonological) and deep (semantic) levels; psychological reality thereof; speaker-hearer plays active role in language interpretation; differences between natural and artificial languages. The mark of transformational grammar is the necessary emphasis on distinguishing the two levels of sentence interpretation. There is the *surface level,* which is related directly to the sentence as we hear it, and the *deep level,* which is related directly to meaning. Chomsky felt that it is the inability of surface structures to indicate semantically significant grammatical relations that has caused transformational grammar to be developed. This transformational generative grammar is a device for pairing the phonetically represented signals of the surface structure of a sentence with the semantic interpretations of the sentence's deep structure. These pairings are mediated by the sentence's syntactic components.

It appears that distinctions between *deep* and *surface* structures in a sentence possess psychological reality and relevance. Since it is easier to recall a particular sentence than a randomization of the words within that sentence, persons do not remember a sentence merely as a string of words (Slobin, 1971). In addition, anomalous sentences are more difficult to recall than meaningful ones. Since one can paraphrase or summarize what one has recently heard without giving or perhaps without being able to give a verbatim report, meaning and form can be stored independently. It would appear that perception of sentence meaning occurs in the *deep* rather than the *surface* structure. Sachs (1967) supported this concept in an experiment which showed that form, which is not relevant to meaning, is normally not retained. When test sentences were heard with no intervening delay, subjects were able to recognize both semantic and syntactic changes. After about twenty-seven seconds' delay, subjects' recognition of syntactic changes (for example, active to passive) was close to that of chance, whereas their recognition of semantic changes remained strong even after about forty-six seconds. Sachs concluded that the meaning of the sentence is derived from the original string of words by an active interpretive process.

The perception of a sentence as a structured string of words (phrase structure) and the Gestalt assumption that a perceptual unit tends to preserve its integrity by resisting interruptions were tested by Fodor and Bever (1965). To prove the psychological reality of phrase structure, they asked their subjects to listen to sentences during which clicks occurred. The subjects were most accurate in locating those clicks which were heard between the major phrases of a sentence. In addition, clicks occurring on either side of the "natural breaks in the sentence" tended to be displaced toward those breaks.

Further research tended to corroborate these findings, indicating that there were no acoustic or pause cues which might have been responsible for the results, but that the results were due to perceiving the language units as corresponding to the constituent phrase structure. It appears that the speaker-hearer (writer-reader?) assigns a perceptual structure to speech sounds on the basis of his knowledge of the rules of language, and so plays an active part in the interpretation of what he hears.

The notion that human language has a transformational structure with surface (phonological) and deep (semantic) levels may be based on the fact that *natural* languages at least are originally transmitted through the auditory medium, a medium which because of its nature requires temporal sequencing and order, and rapid fading of the message units (Slobin, 1971). Computer, mathematical, and other *invented* languages do not possess these peculiar dual structures, probably because these *artificial* languages are essentially transmitted via visual media and so can be scanned and rescanned as needed. A resultant current psycholinguistic concept is that speech and language perceptions involve two memories, short-term and long-term. In short-term memory one has time to compute only the surface structure of a sentence, which is then passed on to a larger memory store. There, without the immediate pressure of rapid fading, the deep structure and corresponding meaning are derived.

Processing grammatical information takes time; the simplest sentence is active-declarative-affirmative, that is, kernel sentence. Savin and Perchonock (1965) showed that the processing of grammatical information can take up space in memory because certain aspects of syntax are used in the remembering process. They quoted the research of McMahon (1963), who showed by measuring the time required to decide whether various sentences were true or false that syntactic features such as negativity and passivity are encoded independently of the other characteristics of a sentence. Times required for decisions regarding passive sentences were longer than for active sentences and negative sentences required longer times than affirmative ones. In addition, there was no interaction between passivity and negativity, in that the increment due to the passive feature was the same regardless of whether the sentence was also negative. McMahon concluded that the subjects probably had to recover something similar to the active, declarative, affirmative sentence (kernel sentence), decide whether that was true, then consider whether the original had been negative.

Savin and Perchonock (1965) demonstrated the role of syntax in organizing sentences into units larger than words. Their prediction, based upon the concept of transformational grammar, was that the "grammatical tags," such as "passive," "negative," or "question," would take up extra space in immediate memory. The subjects memorized sentences of various grammatical types. Each sentence was followed by a list of words, which was also to be memorized. The results indicated that the more complex the grammatical structure of the sentence, the fewer words are recalled in addition to the sentences. The largest number of words remembered followed the memorized active-declarative sentence; the smallest number of words remembered came after the negative-passive-interrogative and emphatic-passive memorized sentences. Savin and Perchonock concluded that various grammatical features are encoded in short-term memory, apart from the rest of the sentence.

The difference between language competence and language performance; ability to use innate rules makes for productivity of language. A distinction is made between *language competence* and *language performance. Competence* is the model of what is assumed to exist in the mind of the ideal speaker-listener (and writer-reader), the mechanism that produces knowledge of language. In addition to the incorporated generative rules of grammar, there is a heuristic component which samples an input sentence and by a series of successive approximations determines the rules used to generate the sentence. The speaker-listener (writer-reader) can formulate all categories of sentences, affirmative, negative, imperative, and so on. He therefore does not have to memorize or imitate each possible sentence but rather, by using his set of innate rules, he can generate the infinite variety of sentences of his native language (Chomsky, 1967). The actual human performance of speaking-understanding (and writing-reading) language does not satisfactorily measure underlying competence. Psycholinguistic variables intervene to distort predictions based on the pure competence model. Such variables include limited memory span, fatigue, decreased attention span, emotional excitement or depression, drug effects, physical well-being, distractibility, and congenitally and developmentally aberrant states.

Critical stages in language development; equipotentiality of cortical tissue in younger children; hearing loss and language development. In animals other than man critical maturational stages in primary socialization and imprinting seem to exist (Scott, 1962). In man critical maturational stages appear to exist, for example, in learning appropriate sex-roles (Lewis et al., 1970). These critical periods occur relatively early in life, when growth and behavioral differentiation undergo rapid organization. The plasticity noted only in the young suggests that further organization with age inhibits reorganization. For example, Penfield and Roberts (1959) stated that after illness or injury has destroyed the speech areas in the dominant left cerebral hemisphere, an aphasic child manifests remarkable relearning ability. Although either a child or an adult may be rendered speechless, the child usually recovers within months, while the adult may or may not recover depending upon the severity of the insult. Examples of completely successful transfer of speech mechanisms from left to right hemisphere in children younger than three or four years are numerous. Lenneberg (1964) discussed the functional equipotentiality of the cortex in infants and children younger than three years. The entire left hemisphere may be incapacitated by agenesis, trauma, infection, or even surgical hemispherectomy for neoplasia. Still, language acquisition will take place provided the insult occurred at a sufficiently early age, was confined to one hemisphere, and did not induce generalized severe mental retardation.

The concept of critical stages in language development is also supported by evidence relating to the time at which hearing is lost. If, for example, an infant is rendered deaf by meningitis within the first year of life, he develops essentially as a deaf-mute, behaving much the same as those infants who are born with familial deafness. Those children who lose their hearing between the ages of three and four years—shortly after they have acquired some language—have a much better prognosis for developing normal language and speech than have those who lose their hearing before that apparently critical period, from eighteen to thirty-six months of age.

During this critical period an infant seems to benefit greatly from short exposures to and practice with language. Fry (1966) stated that in the normally hearing child, development of the phonological system is complete and fairly well-established by five to seven years of age. The normal development of this system is dependent upon the complex interactions of auditory and kinesthetic feedback, without which the motor skills of speech cannot be satisfactorily acquired.

Fry believed that the clearly greater success in speech development of English than of American or Continental European deaf children has to do with very early diagnosis and training. In England deaf children are provided with hearing aids as early as age two years, and are given intensive sound training long before school begins. It appears that in America such attempts do not begin seriously until age four or five years, well after the critical period for language acquisition.

Holm and Kunze (1969), however, indicated that the critical period for speech and language acquisition may at least partially extend beyond the eighteen to thirty-six month age span. Periodic lack of auditory-sensory stimulation experienced during phases of intermittent conductive hearing loss due to frequent episodes of otitis media in children between five and nine years of age resulted in significant delays in language and speech skills, as judged by comparison with an appropriate control group. It may be noted that no significant differences between the affected children and controls were found in assessments of primarily visual and motor skills.

The neuropsychopathologies interfering with
the normal development of language

Normal speech and language functioning are disrupted
by any of a broad spectrum of neuropathologic and psychopathologic states including the aphasias, the autisms,
the schizophrenias, the language delays, the cerebral
palsies, the epilepsies, the retardations, and the conditions of deafness and mutism. Motivational factors and
malingering have to be considered as well. Two clinical
entities described relatively recently include dysfunctions
in speech and language which seem to be uniquely and
clearly related to specific etiologic factors.

*Histidinemia: an inborn error of metabolism specifi-
cally affecting speech and language?* In 1908 Garrod described albinism, alkaptonuria, cystinuria, and pentosuria
as prototypes of a group of inborn errors of metabolism.
Since then, more than one hundred such syndromes have
been reported including phenylketonuria and histidinemia.
La Du (1972) reviewed fifty-four case histories of patients
with histidinemia, a genetic metabolic disorder, first described in 1961, which is due to an inherited deficiency
of the enzyme histidase, the lack of that activity causing
markedly reduced conversion of histidine to urocanic acid.
This autosomal recessive trait permits histidine to accumulate in blood, cerebrospinal fluid, and urine. The latter
reacts positively with ferric chloride, causing a murky
green color. The earlier reports indicated that this inherited
disease showed an unusual predilection to interfere with
speech and language functioning but that generally the intelligence quotients of the subjects were within normal
limits, in contradistinction to those of patients with phenylketonuria. Although the testing procedures were not
well-standardized with regard to speech and language,
shortened auditory memory and delayed speech patterns
were noted in most patients. As more cases were reported
and described it appeared that more than half of the

patients show some form of mental retardation, and that
more than half also manifest various types of delayed
language and speech development. Some patients' diseases
overlap and belong to both of these diagnostic categories.
To further complicate the picture, Levy et al. (1974), in a
prospective study (completed) routinely screening 400,488
newborns by filter paper chromatography of urine speci-
mens, found histidinemia in 20 newborns, a frequency of
1:20,000, whereas the frequency of phenylketonuria was
1:15,000. None of the infants received any form of treatment such as a low-histidine diet, yet after follow-up
periods averaging seven to eight years, none showed
mental subnormality and only one manifested speech and
language maldevelopment. Levy et al. concluded that there
might be two forms of histidinemia, one of which is
clinically benign. It is also possible that excessive
amounts of metabolites may accumulate and ultimately
have a deleterious effect upon certain neurophysiologically based *critical stages* of development. Diurnal and
perhaps other temporal variations in metabolite levels
might account for the two different clinical pictures described by Levy and coworkers.

*Aberrations in kinesthetic feedback causing language
and speech dysfunctions.* Malfunctioning of kinesthetic
feedback processes is another possible cause of speech
(and language?) production deficits. MacNeilage et al.
(1967) described a seventeen-year-old girl who had had
marked difficulties with swallowing and chewing, as well
as a severe speech (and language?) production deficit
since early childhood. Yet her ability to decode incoming
speech and language approached normalcy. She had a
full-scale Wechsler Intelligence Scale for Children (WISC)
IQ score of ninety and her hearing was within normal
limits. After extensive investigation, including electromy-
ography and cinefluorography, it was concluded that the
severe speech (and language?) production deficits were
not primarily of motor origin, but rather resulted from

congenital inability to obtain somesthetic feedback information from the buccal mucosa of the oral cavity. Such somesthetic feedback information is necessary for the learning of the patterns of spatial distribution and temporal modulation of muscle contractions accompanying one's own normal speech. In contrast to the lack of evidence for direct damage to the motor system in this patient, there was a great deal to suggest damage to the mechanism of somesthetic sensibility, in that stereognosis, sensitivity to painful stimuli, tactile localization, and two-point discrimination were all impaired, especially about the face, mouth, and lips. It appears likely that sensory information which accompanies early attempts at speech gesture is necessary in order for the speaker to identify the more successful attempts at communication and accordingly modify his program for future speech (and language?) production.

As with other fully developed syndromes describing complete panels of dysfunctioning, formes-frustes (an incomplete form of a syndrome) may exist (for example, hypoparathyroidism, pseudo-hypoparathyroidism, pseudo-pseudo-hypoparathyroidism; Rosenthal, 1961). Within the differential diagnostic spectrum of the dysphasias-dysphagias, somesthesia should be considered.

Terminological confusion due to approaches from various disciplines; differences between speech *and* language *problems; assessing aberrant language development by specific tests of grammatical competence.* Disorders of speech and language are among the clinically described entities within the framework of the minimal cerebral dysfunctions (Bakwin, 1965). It is not only that confusion has attended attempts to clinically and neurophysiologically categorize the spectrum of difficulties, but also that problems of nomenclature have arisen from interdisciplinary differences in terminology. As a result a number of diagnostic categories are not specific and tend to overlap, for example, language delays, auditory sequencing difficulties, agrammatism, syntactical disorders, speech problems, auditory discrimination problems, categories of expressive and receptive aphasia, autism and autism-like states, speech irregularities, and so forth. In recent years the differentiations between speech disabilities, such as motoric-articulatory end-organ malfunction, and language difficulties, such as underlying psycholinguistic-developmental disabilities, have come to the fore (Menyuk, 1964; Lee, 1966). By assiduous longitudinal observation and categorization, hierarchical standardizations of appropriate grammatical stages for age within language maturation have been developed. Lee, by creating Developmental Sentence Types, was able to distinguish and contrast normal and deviant syntactic development in her subjects. Children with "atypical speech" often also have "atypical language" development. For both diagnosis and appropriate choice of method of remediation, it is necessary to distinguish phonemic problems from those of morphology, syntactics, and semantics. As an example of terminological confusion, one of Lee's subjects who manifested deviant syntactic development was also diagnosed by different specialists as having "a forme-fruste of cerebral palsy-ataxic type with a slight intention tremor and a slight Romberg," "sensory and motor aphasia," and "on the Illinois Test of Psycholinguistic Abilities (ITPA), perceptual problems considerably more severe in audition than in vision" (Lee, 1967). Because of possible lack of "readiness" in academic skills as well, the child repeated kindergarten.

Menyuk, using a generative model of grammar, compared subjects with "infantile speech" and normals. Language samples were gathered, including elicited imitation sentences of different transformational types. The term "infantile speech" seemed to be a misnomer because at no age level did grammatical production and competence of a child with "infantile speech" closely match that of the normal controls, again pointing up the difference between speech and language.

Elicited imitations have been used for psycholinguistic assessment (Rosenthal, 1970) of children with minimal brain dysfunction (MBD). Elicited imitations are not the simple sentence repetitions they seem to be; they involve decoding, storage, and encoding processes. Elicited imitations were found to be useful tools for testing linguistic competence in normal children and in children with MBD (syndromes of distractibility-hyperactivity, the dyslexias-dysgraphias, syndromes of motor-perceptual dysfunctions, and language delays). Definitive differences between the two groups were noted, especially in sentence completions and transformational changes from affirmative to negative, in that hesitations, repetitions, substitutions, and omissions were significantly more common in the elicited imitations of those subjects who had MBD.

II

Origins of
Human Language

*Language and symbolic behavior; intermediate
stages of verbalization with gesture; the symbol
of symbols, written language*

Many tend to view the origins of speech and language
as part of a larger developing faculty—that of symbolic
behavior (d'Alviella, 1894; Sapir, 1921; White, 1949;
Critchley, 1970a). White (1949) considered that this
creative and referential capacity for symbolism is the
ability to bestow value or meaning upon an item. Signs
indicate physical things or events. Symbols *represent*
physical things or events and, unlike signs, are not restricted to the confines of immediate time and place.

Sapir believed that language is a purely human, non-
instinctive method of communicating ideas, emotions, and
desires by means of a system of voluntarily produced
symbols. Language almost certainly arose as a vocal-
auditory system. An intermediary and subsidiary method
of speech symbolism is perceived when the sounds of
language are replaced by the visual images of the articula-
tions which correspond to the sound, for example the
reading of the lips which deaf-mutes learn to do so well
in apprehending "speech" and language.

In evolutionary development when the forelimbs of primates were no longer needed for locomotion, prehension became possible; so, in addition, did more deliberate pantomime. Given the rich antecedent gestural methods of animal communication, the theory was developed of an intermediate homo alalus as a stage of early man who communicated by gestures but not by utterances. Critchley (1970a) suggested that it is more probable that homo alalus never really existed, but that gesture and verbalization grew side by side as elaborated symbols on the way to the appearance of homo loquens. Perhaps a prototype of this relationship is seen in the almost universal form of the request for silence—placing the forefinger vertically against the lips, through which a hiss is emitted.

Next in evolutionary sequence, the most important of visual speech symbolisms are those systems of delicately adjusted movements which result in graphic methods of recording speech. Written forms are secondary symbols of the spoken ones, or symbols of symbols.

Nonverbal communication

Linguistic-kinesic interactions, normal and pathological

Nonverbal forms of expression and communication are ubiquitous. According to anecdotal information received by Critchley (1970a), gesture and verbal language seem to flourish especially well together among the ethnic and cultural groups of Southern Europe, but motion and language appear to be bound together in all human interactions. In studied audiovisual tapes, Scheflen (1964) found significant linguistic-kinesic interactions and correspondences between patient and therapist. Condon (1967) found linguistic-kinesic units in which there was a relatively exact correlation between boundary points of speech segments and those of body motion, indicating a self-synchrony in the integrity of the behavior of the single organism. In addition there were units of interactional synchrony which revealed a precise synchrony between speaker and interactant. Interestingly and significantly there were very few adventitious body movements except in several schizophrenic and aphasic patients. In studying communicative behavioral units as a whole, Brosin (1967) suggested future investigations of visceral functions—hair positioning and secretions, skin color and blanching, pilomotor erection of hair, sweating, arterial pulsations, pupillary size, and respiratory rate and depth.

Behavioral scientists have become aware that contradictory signals and propositions may exist as responses at different levels (lexical, linguistic, kinesic, visceral) within one person. Since all of the contradictory information might be received in human interaction, much confusion in interpersonal relations might result, perhaps especially in child-rearing and in therapeutic situations (Brosin, 1967).

Just as there are only twenty-six letters in the English alphabet, with a resultant number of acceptable phoneme combinations, Scheflen estimated that there are no more than about thirty traditional American gestures. These kinesic units for nondeviant acculturated Americans occur in a limited and standard number of situations.

Nonverbal kinesic universals as analogues
of language universals

Ekman et al. (1969) stressed the existence of pancultural elements in facial displays of emotion, suggesting that just as there are postulated language universals, there may also be nonverbal kinesic universals. Subjects native to literate (United States, Brazil, Japan) cultures and preliterate (New Guinea, Borneo) cultures, when presented with photographs of the face, chose the predicted emotion among the offered alternatives happiness, surprise, fear, anger, disgust-contempt, and sadness. Agreement, however, was higher in the samples from the literate cultures. Noting the pancultural element in facial displays of emotions as the association between facial muscular movements and discrete primary emotions, Ekman et al. suggested that cultures may still differ with respect to rules for controlling the display of emotion, and with respect to behavioral consequences.

In addition to partial and total body movements, linguistic pitch markers are often accompanied by kinesic postural markers involving head, hand, and/or eyelids to indicate statements, questions, or continuation of speech (Scheflen, 1964). Ekman and Friesen (1972) devised a classification of nonverbal behavior with relation to hand movements but indicated that distinctions among the classes—emblems, illustrators, and adaptors—apply also to leg and facial movements. The classifications are based on origin, usage, and coding; they convert a vague area of behavior into data that can be examined quantitatively.

Nonverbal systems which replace verbal systems

Pantomime systems totally replace articulate speech as media of communication in special circumstances, for examples, in American Sign Language (the sign language of deaf-mutes, or dactylology), in Oriental and Polynesian dances, in occupational sign languages, in sign languages of secret societies, in sign languages of geographically close yet linguistically different tribes, in sign languages of certain monastic orders that allow articulate speech only at specified times, and in the sign language of the Bushman hunters of South Africa.

Other systems of human communication exist which are not really nonverbal systems because in a sense they are based upon words, for example braille, Morse code, shorthand, signaling (military), drum messages (Africa and Melanesia) and the whistled languages of Mexico, Turkey, West Africa, and the French Pyrenees as well as the whistled Silbo of the Canary Islands (Critchley, 1970a).

Historical antecedents and cultural
equivalents of language

Critchley (1970a) presented the problem of the historical origin of language as resolving itself into a search for the earliest indications of symbolic behaviors in man as the immediate precursors of speech. In efforts to trace the origin of human language investigators and theorists have attempted to integrate evidence from the interrelations among cultural, language, auditory-vocal, social, and neurophysiological development.

From an evolutionary point of view, perhaps the most constant cofactor of the development of language in man has to do with the establishment of intergroup cooperation and the fundamentals of human society. If acceptable expressions of culture and symbolic behavior are the fashioning of elaborate tools (Washburn, 1960), the use of fire and clothing, evidence of organized hunts and ceremonial burials, manifestations of religious or magical practices, and the skillful cave paintings of El Castillo and Altamira (Spain) and Lascaux (France), then one would predict that language is at least as old as Cro-Magnon times, the period from 35,000 to 10,000 years ago, corresponding geologically to the Last Ice Age and archaeologically to the Late Paleolithic Age.

Anthropological investigations of skull size and development

Critchley (1970a) cited the anatomical studies of Keith and Tilney, who suggested that the faculty of speech could be traced as far back as Neanderthal man or to at least 50,000 years ago, corresponding archaeologically to the Middle Paleolithic Age and geologically to the Upper Pleistocene Age. Keith's studies suggested that the skull of Neanderthal man was of such nature that the left hemisphere was more massive than the right, suggesting cerebral dominance. Tilney's studies of Neanderthal skulls showed a "well-developed" auditory area, indicated by the increased depth of the parietal fossae. Cultural evidence for Neanderthal man's language abilities also exists—tool-making (sharpened flints and arrow heads), the use and control of fire, the practice of cookery, and organized elephant hunts were part of Neanderthal man's life pattern—all denoting some degree of conceptual and symbolic thinking. Studies by Tilney of the skulls of Pithecanthropus erectus (Java man) and Sinanthropus pekinensis (Peking man) suggested that the left frontal area of these brains was larger than the right, suggesting dominance and implying that perhaps some language abilities already existed about 500,000 years ago (Lower Paleolithic Age archaeologically, Middle Pleistocene Age geologically).

Measurements of the left and right cerebral hemispheres

Definitive anatomical studies to ascertain possible differences between the left and right cerebral hemispheres have been made only recently. Geschwind and Levitsky (1968) found marked anatomical asymmetries between the upper surfaces of human left and right temporal lobes in one hundred adult human brains obtained at postmortem examination and free of significant pathologic conditions. Unfortunately, handedness data were not available, but Geschwind and Levitsky assumed that their one hundred cases must have been overwhelmingly of subjects who were left-brain dominant for speech, in view of the fact that ninety-three percent of an average adult population are right-handed, while ninety-six percent are left-brained for speech. They found that the planum temporale, the area immediately posterior to Heschl's gyrus of the temporal lobe, was larger on the left than on the right in sixty-five percent of the brains, but it was larger on the right than on the left in only eleven percent. While Heschl's gyrus contains the primary auditory cortex, the planum temporale contains cortical areas of auditory association which on the left constitute the classic area of Wernicke, a region known from anatomical findings in aphasic patients and from stimulation studies during neurosurgical procedures to be of major importance in language function.

Witelson and Pallie (1973) substantiated the work of Geschwind and Levitsky by data showing anatomical asymmetries between the left and right cerebral hemispheres correlating with the clinically known functional asymmetries. Both linear and area measurements showed that the left planum temporale was significantly larger than the right in the sixteen adult and fourteen infant (eleven neonatal) brains measured. Witelson and Pallie stressed that the anatomic asymmetries, found especially in the neonates, lend further support to the concept that language is a preprogrammed, inborn, biological capacity, rather than a result of learning from the environment. Interestingly, the anatomic differences were less marked in the males than in the females.

Evolutionary aspects of cerebral
hemispheric lateralization

The phenomena of cerebral hemispheric lateralization, dominance, and handedness, and their relation to language and speech development have been discussed for many years. Subirana (1964) cited early observers who assumed that lower forms of the phylogenetic scale manifested lateral symmetry. But snails can be divided according to the orientation of the spirals of their shells into dextrals and sinistrals; the dextrals are more numerous. Heterochylia (asymmetry of claws) is one of the most pronounced characteristics of the crustaceae. Although the numerical relation between dextrals and sinistrals in a given species of crustaceae is not clear, it is interesting that a phenomenon of compensatory regeneration occurs at times perhaps related to "shifting dominance" in humans (if left hemisphere damage occurs early enough in life in humans, the right hemisphere takes over language function). When the crustacean has lost its large claw, the remaining small one grows into a large claw, while a new small claw grows on the side of loss. The hunter observes that his dog uses a preferred paw for pointing out game. Eighty percent of rats seem to prefer one paw for taking food, generally using the right, although there is a high percentage of ambidexterity. Chimpanzees seem to prefer one hand or the other, equally right or left.

Monkeys, too, were found to be characterized by one-handed dominance in manipulation of a problem box to extricate food, but the degree of dominance varied in diverse animals. Interestingly, the lateral preference of monkeys was more marked in natural life conditions than in captivity.

Contradictory evidence exists with relation to the handedness of Stone Age man. Subirana suggested that dextrals were as frequent as sinistrals, because flints fitting the right hand were as frequent as flints fitting the left hand. Ancient cave drawings showed a preponderance of left hands holding the bow and arrow; the significance of this observation is not clear.

Handedness, cerebral dominance,
and language function

Although most authorities recognize a higher incidence of left-handedness, ambidexterity, and mixed dominance (for example, right-handed, left-footed, right-eyed; left-handed, right-footed, right-eyed) in patients with MBD and in those with dyslexia (to be defined later), opinions vary from that of Goldberg (1968), who believes that there is very little relation, to that of Orton (1937), who believed that the cause of dyslexia is the lack of establishment of cerebral dominance as seen clinically by left-handedness, ambidexterity, or mixed dominance. Broca first drew attention to the three-way relationship among cerebral dominance, language, and handedness when he ascribed speech dominance to the cerebral hemisphere contralateral to the preferred hand. Adherence to the belief in the correspondence between handedness and speech and language laterality has waned. Current thought is that a presumed one-to-one correlation between handedness and hemispheric dominance for language does not exist (McNeil and Hamre, 1974). Geschwind (1971) observed that while aphasias in association with lesions of the right hemisphere are extremely rare, occurring less often than one in one hundred cases among right-handed persons, at least sixty percent of the aphasias in left-handed persons result from lesions in the left hemisphere. The consensus is that almost all right-handed persons and approximately two-thirds of left-handed persons have a language-dominant left cerebral hemisphere (McNeil and Hamre, 1974).

Goldberg (1968) indicated that there are at least two types of left-handedness: 1) physiologic and genetic, and 2) pathologic, which may be the result of subtle brain damage in which a genetically predisposed right-handed person finds it functionally more convenient to use the left. Handedness, leggedness, and eyedness can be tested for clinically, but, as Geschwind noted, a one-to-one correlation between these and hemispheric dominance for language does not exist.

Taking into account that the word "left" is the English equivalent of Latin *sinister*, Critchley (1970a) indicated that many sinistrals find themselves compelled to adopt unnatural right-handed techniques simply because certain tools are manufactured for dextral use (scissors, hockey sticks). In addition, observations of left-handed youngsters trying to write from their own thoughts or to dictation in a written language that goes from left to right show that their writing hand is clumsily sprawled sequentially over what they have written, making it difficult for them to see what they have just set down.

Testing for cerebral dominance has engendered much interest in the last few years. Among the techniques used have been dichotic (simultaneous presentation of different auditory stimuli to each ear) and dicoptic (simultaneous stimulation of right and left visual fields) and the sodium amytal method of Wada (McNeil and Hamre, 1974). Recently, neurophysiological investigations using refined electroencephalographic (EEG) techniques are shedding light not so much on cerebral "dominance" as on lateralized and specialized cerebral functions.

Noting that brain blood flow is regulated by neuronal metabolic activity, Ingvar and Schwartz (1974) have used a regional cerebral blood flow (rCBF) technique to obtain quantitative maps of hemisphere regions during speech and reading. In a psychiatric clientele, rCBF in the left hemisphere of ten right-handed neurologically normal patients, and in the right hemisphere of two right-handed and one left-handed patients, was studied by means of a thirty-two-detector device. Measurements were made at rest, during simple speech and reading, and during contralateral hand-arm work. Speech or reading did not change *total* mean hemispheric blood flow or oxygen uptake, but the typical rCBF resting pattern changed markedly. During rest the highest flows were precentral; the lowest, postcentral. During speech the highest flows were in the premotor, rolandic, anterior- and mid-Sylvian regions of the cerebral cortex. The same changes occurred during reading. In addition, post-central flow increased. In the three right hemispheres studied, speech was accompanied by postcentral blood flow decrease. These studies demonstrated that speaking and reading activate substantial parts of the middle and lower rolandic region, in addition to the upper, anterior, and (apparently in lesser degree) the posterior speech cortex in the dominant hemisphere. This pattern differs from the one recorded during abstract thinking and problem solving, in which frontal and postcentral associational areas are more activated. Involvement of the posterior speech cortex (Wernicke's area) appeared surprisingly limited, especially during reading.

III

Written Language and Reading

Definitions, historical antecedents

Written language (and reading) probably came into existence at a much later time in the history of man than did the language of the vocal-auditory channel. Speech and gesture are of momentary duration and therefore restricted in time. Speech and gesture also function adequately only among communicators who are in close proximity, and are therefore restricted in relation to space. Writing and reading, being systems of human communication by means of visible, conventional, graphic symbols, release man from these two restrictions. The pictures in the Cro-Magnon caves may represent the earliest methods of passing along information by graphic means. But the explicitly realistic pictures of bison, reindeer, horses, and man are accompanied by puzzling markings on the walls of caves including silhouettes of human hands, abstract patterns of colored dots and lines, as well as boxes, bell shapes, and barbed signs. Perhaps the latter were akin to systems of mnemonic signs which have been developed and persist in various parts of the world to keep accounts. These include tally or counting sticks, pebbles in a sack, as well as the *quipu* of the Peruvian Incas, who had no written language. The *quipus* were cords to which were attached, at meaningful intervals, cords of various lengths and colors knotted in specific ways. These were created and kept for the purposes of remembering tax and historical records, and even for the transmission of messages (Ogg, 1948).

Development of alphabets

Aided by the proper uses of the wedge and soft clay, the reed pen and papyrus, the chisel and stone, written language passed through stages and combinations of stages—ideographic, pictographic, hieroglyphic (polyphonic and homophonic), hieratic, cuneiform, rebus symbols, syllabic, and alphabetic (Laird, 1953). Our modern English alphabet can be traced back from the Latin to the Greek to the Phoenician to several more ancient Semitic alphabets. The pre-Greek alphabets were essentially made up of consonants.

In addition to introducing vowel symbols the Greeks made several practical changes affecting the direction of writing. The direction of writing had included up-and-down formats; it may have been dictated by what fit best into an available space. Semitic writing even today reads from right to left, a convention which may perhaps indicate that its forerunner was a carved script, designed for the convenience of the right-handed engraver.

Early Greek inscriptions also ran from right to left, but a period of experimentation followed, during which the direction alternated at each successive line. This method was called *boustrophedon*, meaning "ox-turning": an ox plows a furrow in a field, turning at the perimeter and plowing the next row in the opposite direction. In conjunction with this, all letters except those which were symmetrical, such as *H* and *M*, were reversed in successive and alternate lines of writing. The restricted left-to-right style was finally adopted because of its simplicity, but did not appear until the beginning of the seventh century B.C. It was obviously better suited to the right-handed scribes of the pen-and-ink era.

The classical Latin alphabet, which came from the Greeks through the Etruscans, contained twenty-three letters. The expansion of *V* into *U* and *W*, and the differentiation of *I* and *J* took place respectively in the tenth and fourteenth centuries of the present era, finally giving the English alphabet twenty-six letters (Ogg, 1948; Cleator, 1961).

During the last 2,500 years hundreds of alphabets have been developed throughout the world. Widely known examples include Brahmi, Pahlavi, Modern Hebrew, Modern Arabic, Armenian, Runic, Phrygian, Ogham, Cyrillic, Glagolitic, Kana, and so forth. Alphabets may be sorted into three main groups according to the methods by which they indicate vowels. In Greek and Latin the vowels are shown as separate signs: *A*, *E*, *I*, *O*, and *U*. In Modern Hebrew and Modern Arabic vowels are indicated by separate diacritical marks under the consonants. In Indic and Ethiopic vowels are indicated by diacritical marks attached to the sign, or by internal modification of the sign.

Transitions between spoken and written language: vernaculars and dialects

Written language was originally developed to release verbal language from the restraints of time and place. Through the years, however, verbal and written language have not been absolutely faithful to one another. Differences between written and spoken language exist at morphologic, syntactic, and semantic levels. Written language usually possesses a wider vocabulary range, is more premeditated and precise, and is governed by stricter rules of grammar and style, although in an eloquent and practiced public speaker the differences between written and spoken language may be less marked. Spoken language has its own advantages because it permits sudden changes in prosodic features, for example, fluctuation of pitch and tempo. Stages between the two include the vernacular, colloquialisms, popular journalism, and the prose of the playwright (Critchley, 1970a).

Dialects or drifts of language arise because two or more groups of persons who originally spoke one language became sufficiently disconnected from the other group or groups, with respect to social, cultural, nationalistic, or religious differences (or with respect to more than one of these), to develop characteristic speech forms (Sapir, 1921). The terms "language stock," "language branch," and "dialect" are relative. At times a dialect may become so well ensconced culturally that newspapers are published in its written form, such as Schweizer-Deutsch. Yet even within a clearly defined geographic area differing language patterns may develop.

Restricted and elaborated language codes

In discussing "restricted" and "elaborated" codes from a sociolinguistic point of view, Bernstein (1964) proposed that members of lower classes command a narrower range of linguistic styles than do the members of higher classes, and that this may affect developmental processes of socialization, cognition, and perhaps motivation. Bernstein noted, however, that although restricted-code speakers are found more often in the lower socioeconomic strata, they are also found in certain upper-class groups.

Models of learning and development: nativist-empiricist conflict

Approaches to the phenomena of learning and development and their dysfunctions have varied, at times to the point of strife. The approach selected has depended upon the individual point of view of the discipline involved. Learning and development and dysfunctions thereof have been represented by partial and complete models stemming from psychology, education, medicine, linguistics, speech and language, audiology, sociology and so forth. Within pschology there have been cognitive, perceptual, behavioristic, information-processing, motivational, developmental, and analytic interpretations.

Mechanical mirror theories

Langer (1969a) discussed learning and development from the point of view of the conceptual polarities, the *mechanical mirror* and the *organic lamp* theories. Central to the mechanical mirror conception of learning and development is the environmentalistic assumption that the source for all psychological phenomena is stimulation from the external world. Langer traced the mechanical mirror conceptions from Plato, Locke, Pavlov, Watson, Hull, and Skinner to those behavioral responses that may be self-produced, as described by Bijou and Baer, an example of which is reminding oneself of the late hour, and those which may be mediated by the child to produce other overt responses, as noted in the work of Berlyne and Kendler and Kendler. This conception of "covert responses" is at the heart of the hypothesis that postulates mechanical mirror reduction of man's higher mental processes (thinking) to primarily physical responses. Langer discussed the concepts of classic and operant conditioning, reinforcement, imitation and social learning, and those mediational stages which govern the child's acquisition of associations of stimuli and responses. The cumulation and strengthening of associations with time constitute learning, development, and memory in the child. Weakening or elimination of these associations, especially in a social context, which may be experimental (Harlow and Harlow,

1962), inadvertent (Spitz, 1945), or purposive (Bowlby, 1966; Ainsworth, 1966), may lead to syndromes of social deprivation, maternal deprivation, hospitalism, anaclitic depression, or failure to thrive. Spitz (1945) indicated that because of the lack of maternal attention received by institutionally reared infants and children, the infection rates and death rates were high and retardation was evident in growth, motor, perceptual, and intellectual areas.

The organic lamp theory

Proponents of the *organic lamp* theory (Langer, 1969b) trace the origins of their concepts to Aristotle's "contemplation" and Descartes' "I think; therefore I am," which propose that much of man's psychological functioning grows out of and is the highest expression of his biological functioning. The underpinnings are genetic, biochemical, and neurophysiological, but the organism must interact with the environment to achieve its full potential. Gesell (1966) stressed that human characteristics are already present in the early stages of fetal and postnatal development. Werner (1948, 1957) adapted the biological principle of orthogenesis in his organismic theory of development, which stressed that as maturation of the organism occurs, states of relative globality and lack of differentiation are replaced and subordinated by novel, more highly integrated, and increasingly hierarchical systems of functioning. Werner felt that from the organism's early sensorimotor experiences with its environment, perceptual-analytic stages and then contemplative-synthetic stages emerge successively in relatively orderly fashion. Neuropathologic and/or psychopathologic aberrations cause regression by dedifferentiation and disintegration of the previously normally developing functionally and structurally hierarchized organizational whole. Interestingly, Langer (1969a) suggested that "normal stages of disequilibrium" might be potent forces in normal development. He postulated alternating stages of disequilibrium or cognitive conflict between the child's functional means and adaptive needs, in response to which *novel* means are developed to serve unsatisfied ends, and *novel* ends are sought after as new functional capacities become operative. Piaget (Piaget, 1963; Flavell, 1963; Baldwin, 1967) has studied aspects of cognitive development through sensorimotor, preconceptual, intuitive, and concrete operations and formal reasoning stages. His is the discipline of genetic epistemology, which compares progressive stages of the child's thoughts with relation to the space, time, logic, and mathematics of the real world. Over many years of gathering data, Piaget and his associates have described how the infant and child learn by developing increasingly complex motor-cognitive-behavioral schemas and how, by the complementary adaptive processes of assimilation and accommodation, they learn that the external world is indeed real, independent of their early perceptions of it, and composed of permanent and changing objects in space and time. Finally, the child must conceptualize that others have the same types of experiences.

Psychoanalytic theories of learning and development

Psychoanalytic theories of learning and development (Freud, 1938; Rapaport, 1959) have to do more with personality and affect in psychosexual and psychosocial senses than specifically with cognition and intellect. Yet there are some similarities between the social learning aspects of stimulus-response theories and psychoanalytic theory, in that both put great weight on the importance of early experiences in life to later behaviors. Erikson (1963), who as an ego psychologist is concerned with personal identity formation, feels that all developmental processes are governed by an epigenetic principle of maturation in critical stages. Pathological development will result if the proper rate or proper sequence of these critical stages undergoes interference.

Models of learning: writing-reading

Schisms in psychology

The manner in which children learn specifically to write and to read has long been a concern of psychology. Hypotheses are many, divergent, and often in direct conflict with one another. They range from the stimulus-response concepts of Thorndike through Hull's addition of intermediate mechanisms, Gestalt psychology's principles as elaborated in Lewinian field-theory and life-space definition, and Hebb's neuropsychological postulates (Rabinovitch, 1959). The motivational approaches to learning to write and read, and the primary neurotic causes for difficulties in this area have been stressed from a psychoanalytical point of view by Pearson (1952) and by Blanchard (1946). Freud (1951) discussed as parts of the psychopathology of everyday life the errors of speech, reading, and writing which one encounters at times and stressed that these were due to unconscious disturbances of our personalities.

Schisms in education

Within institutions of higher learning there are marked disagreements at times between the departments of Education and Special Education, concerning the teaching of reading and writing. Arguments are current about the "phonics method" versus the "sight-see method" versus the multisensorial approach. Some believe that barring mental retardation, psychopathology, lack of motivation, malingering, an inadequate educational opportunity, or dysfunctions of vision and hearing, all children should be capable of learning to read adequately. Others are of the opinion that individualization of instruction for each pupil is not only democratic but also a realistic approach, and a necessity because individual differences among human beings with relation to cognitive and personality styles are so marked (Neill, 1960).

*Associationistic approaches to the normal development
of the writing and reading processes: Gibson's theories;
unit structure of speech determines structure of
writing system; differentiation of graphic symbols
(Gibson's first stage); distinctive features
of graphemes and phonemes*

The word "reading" derives from the medieval English *reden*, "to advise, interpret, or read." It means "to receive, or take in the sense of, letters or symbols by scanning," and "to understand the meaning of written or printed matter" (Webster, 1971). Gibson (1965) analyzed reading as a learning process, from the point of view of the experimental psychologist. Her definition of the reading process included these characteristics: "It is receiving communication; it is making discriminative responses to graphic symbols; it is decoding graphic symbols to speech; and it is getting meaning and the printed page." Since a writing system must correspond to the spoken one, and since in human development speech precedes writing, the framework and unit structure of speech essentially determines the structure of the writing system. Gibson believed that as a child begins his progression from spoken to written language, three phases which are sequential yet overlapping are to be considered. The first has to do with the differentiation of graphic symbols. In learning to make a discriminative response to printed characters, the child must be able to work with differentiating features which will not vary under the transformations of size, brightness, and perspective, as well as transformations relating to different typefaces and handwritings.

Money (1962) agreed with Gibson, and stressed that success with the alphabet requires that the reader override at times the principle of object constancy (invariance). It is true that a picture of an object such as a cup, turned about, still represents a cup; the significance of that cup remains constant despite an inconstancy of the configuration of the perceptual sign. But a "b" reversed is a "d";

inverted, it is a "p"; both reversed and inverted, it is a "q"; and nearly a handwritten "9" and a "g." In a series of imaginative experiments Gibson and her research group investigated how children differentiate written symbols. She first used letter-like substitutes. Variants were constructed from created standard figures, artificial letter-like forms comparable to printed Roman capitals. Transformations to be discriminated included line-to-curve, rotations and reversals, as well as transformations relating to break and close, and to perspective. Working with children aged four to eight years, Gibson et al. noted that the visual discrimination of these letter-like forms improved from age four to eight, but that some transformations were more difficult to discriminate than others, and that improvement occurred at different rates for different transformations. Even the youngest subjects had few problems with break or close, but errors with perspective transformations were still numerous in the eight-year-olds. Errors relating to rotation, reversal, and line-to-curve were high at age four but dropped almost to zero by age eight. The experiment was replicated with the same transformations of real letters with a five-year-old group, with closely similar results.

The next study had to do with assessing the *distinctive features* of the letters, those features that enable a child to perceive each letter as unique. The assessment of distinctive features was greatly influenced by the analysis of *distinctive features* of phonemes of Jakobson and Halle (1956). A table of features, each in binary opposition, yields a unique pattern for each phoneme so that any one is distinguishable from all others by its pattern of attributes. Distinctive features appear to be language universals, since different languages use the universal collection of distinctive features to set up diverse sound categories (Slobin, 1971). Examples of distinctive features are whether a phoneme is a vowel or a consonant, whether it is a continuous sound or a single puff of air, and whether it is produced with or without vibrations of the vocal cords (voiced or voiceless consonants). In each of the pairs of sounds *b-p*, *d-t*, *g-k*, *z-s*, the position of the tongue and teeth is the same. The only difference is that when one pronounces *b*, *d*, *g*, and *z* the vocal cords vibrate, and when one pronounces *p*, *t*, *k*, and *s* they do not. In English aspiration occurs with *p*, *t*, and *k* (voiceless stops) when they occur at the beginning of a word such as *pin*, but aspiration does not occur with the sounds in English when they are part of an initial consonant cluster such as in *spin*.

Gibson et al. believed that children, as they develop, learn those distinctive features or dimensions of difference which are critical for differentiating letters. The investigators drew up a set of distinctive features for letters which they speculated must be relational in the sense that each feature presented a contrast that was invariant under certain transformations and must yield a unique pattern for each letter. Examples of distinctive features were straight segment, curve, intersection, redundancy and discontinuity, and so forth. The set should be reasonably economical. Gibson et al. predicted that the tested children should with greatest frequency confuse those letters which had the smallest number of feature differences. The results generally supported the predictions and especially corroborated the choice of the curve-straight and obliqueness variables, suggesting that these features may have priority in the discrimination process. In the historical development of alphabets, perhaps certain letters have naturally persisted because of their highly differentiated qualities, diminishing the chance of error in writing or reading them.

Continuing their studies Gibson et al. inferred that while children probably learn prototypes of letter shapes, the prototypes themselves are not the original basis for differentiation. The most relevant kind of training for discrimination is practice that provides experience for the characteristic differences which distinguish the set of items. Features that are actually distinctive for letters could be emphasized by presenting letters in contrast pairs.

Cognitive approaches to the normal
development of the writing and reading
processes: Neisser; two levels of analysis:
1) the formation of segregated objects,
2) act of focal attention-figural synthesis
(constructive synthetic cognitive activity)

Neisser (1966) in his overview indicated that the Gibson group assumed that letters are recognized by a feature-analysis process. Neisser believed that pattern recognition in general involves a hierarchy of feature-analyzers and that a theory which includes only parallel processing, whether of features or of parts, is not really adequate. For Neisser, in an input situation involving several figures at one time, the number of possible configurations is so very large that a wholly parallel mechanism giving a different output for each of them is "inconceivable." Because he believed that even a mechanical recognition system must include some way of selecting portions of the incoming information for detailed analysis, Neisser postulated the existence of two levels of analysis: 1) the preattentive mechanisms, which form segregated objects and help to direct further processing, and 2) the act of focal attention, which makes more sophisticated figural syntheses of the chosen object. Our perceptions of the detailed properties and features of a figure are in a sense "optional"; hence the process of focal attention is a constructive, synthetic activity rather than a purely analytic one, that is, one *builds* an appropriate visual object.

Grapheme-phoneme decoding (Gibson's second
stage); processing of higher order units—
spelling and morphological patterns of
language (Gibson's third stage)

Gibson's group expressed the opinion that when the graphemes are reasonably discriminable from one another, the decoding process becomes possible, a process which has to do with the association of a graphic stimulus with the appropriate spoken response—the traditional stimulus-response paradigm or a type of paired-associate learning. Several experiments yielded data indicating that it is possible to learn to read words without learning the component letter-sound correspondences. But transfer to new words depends on the use of these correspondences. After the grapheme-phoneme decoding procedure is learned, the child attains competence in reading by gathering skill in the processing of higher order units—the spelling and morphological patterns of the language. Gibson, however, had to deal with the variable as well as the constant letter-sound relationships of English.

The irregularity of English orthography;
corrective teaching by color coding; using
the Initial Teaching Alphabet (ITA)

English is *phonetic* in the sense that separate sounds of the language are represented graphically by printed symbols, in contradistinction to the ideographs used in China and the ideographic Kanji used at times in Japan. In English, there are about forty-eight *phonemes*, of which seventeen are vowels, thirty-one consonants. The forty-eight phonemes are represented by only twenty-six letters or combinations of letters. Therefore, the phoneme-to-grapheme association system in English is not fully systematic; some would say that it is confused and therefore it is said that the *orthography* of the English language is highly irregular. In contrast, some languages such as Spanish, Russian, and the Kana script of Japanese have a very regular phoneme-to-grapheme association system or orthography (Bannatyne, 1973). Bannatyne viewed reading as an essentially auditory-vocal process. He agreed in part with Gibson, when he indicated that children who find it difficult to learn to read do so because they cannot remember the phoneme-to-grapheme coding system. The irregular orthography of the English language is so unsystematic that many children cannot cope with its complexity without help. In those children with reading disability Bannatyne perceived underlying deficits in auditory sequencing, memory, discrimination, and phoneme blending. Bannatyne's research of the reading process indicated to him that the only beneficial way to regularize English orthography is to use a limited system of color coding in the vowels, combined with a psycholinguistic *multisensory approach* to the teaching of reading, writing, and spelling. After all, he argued, if the language is phonetic in the sense that its phonemes are coded, how can purely visual techniques constitute an efficient teaching method? Bannatyne discussed the Initial Teaching Alphabet (ITA) developed by Sir James Pitman and John A. Downing. This is an attempt to create a new alphabet of forty-three characters, some traditional, some new, to establish a more regular grapheme-to-phoneme match. However, the ITA, because it is primarily a reading system, does not lend itself to fast cursive writing. Furthermore, newspapers, signs, and books are printed in traditional orthography, to which those who learn the ITA must still return. Gibson found no hard evidence to suggest that later transfer from the ITA to traditional reading and spelling patterns with more variable component correspondence was facilitated by beginning with only constant ones. In addition, Gibson quoted studies which compared the effects of learning variable and constant letter-sound relationships, whose results indicated that initiating the task with a variable list created an expectation of learning that was set for variability of correspondence, which was transferable to new learning.

The critical unit of language for the reading
process: the spelling pattern (Gibson);
spelling patterns or words as Gestalts (Neisser)

For Gibson and her group the critical unit of language for the reading process is the spelling pattern, which is de-

fined by them as a letter-group that has an invariant relationship with a phonemic pattern. This relevant graphic
unit is a functional unit of one or more letters in a given
position within the word which is in correspondence with
a specified pronunciation in English. Within the immediate
span of visual perception meaning is less effective in
structuring written material than is good spelling to sound
correspondence. Real words, which are both meaningful
and, as strings of letters, structured in accordance with
English spelling patterns, are more easily perceived than
nonword pronounceable strings of letters. But Gibson's
tachistoscopic studies indicated that nonword pronounceable strings of letters, such as *BIM*, are more easily perceived than meaningful but unpronounceable letter-strings
such as *IBM*. Neisser (1967) held that pronounceability
does not necessarily confer unity, because a cluster of
letters cannot be pronounced until after it has been
identified. Assuming that the critical variable in this
process is the frequency with which a grapheme-phoneme
coincidence is experienced, the Gibson hypothesis asserts
that as each spelling pattern in the word is recognized,
the subject produces the corresponding verbal unit. These
strings of sub-vocally spoken units, either real words or
pronounceable pseudo-words, arise in this way. Herein is
a theory that integrates perception and verbal processes.
Neisser saw this as an isomorphism, in the sense of that
term which is employed in Gestalt psychology. Neisser
noted that the theory does not account for errors, especially those which have to do with seeing the word as a
whole which happens to be inappropriate. Neisser suggested
that a feature-analyzer which is sensitive to the global-
stimulus property of a spelling pattern must also exist. Reviewing a series of experiments, he stressed that past
experiences (preceding exposures to the same word) affect
figural-visual synthesis. To perceive words as wholes or as
spelling patterns is to invoke a process of synthesis based
on a concatenation of features. Neisser proposed that the

subject engages in two related constructive acts: (1) he synthesizes a visual figure which may be the word as a whole *or* a spelling pattern, and (2) he constructs a verbal sequence.

Inventory memory in reading:
Money's case of hyperlexia

Money (1962) viewed the whole word-spelling pattern dichotomy in a temporal manner when he stressed that all reading vocabulary for the accomplished, speedy reader, eventually becomes sight-recognition vocabulary. What Money called *inventory memory* and how it may exist as such was dramatically described in one of his cases. The patient was mentally defective because of congenital hypothyroidism, but manifested relative hyperlexia. At age twelve years this girl, whose WISC Verbal Score was seventy-six, Performance Score sixty-one, Full Score sixty-six, could read with good word recognition and comprehension (she was not parroting) at levels far above her IQ scores. Her inventory memory as a discrete cognitive talent was manifested by her ability to recall all telephone numbers and addresses used by her family, all hymns and their page numbers in the church hymnal, and all arithmetic tables.

The relation between information
processing and cognitive development

Neisser stated that by definition, to identify a word or a letter is to pronounce its name in inner or outer speech and thus to store it in verbal immediate memory. Neimark (1971) related maturational stages of information processing to Piagetian stages of cognitive development, especially stressing that as one grows older not only analyzing but also "memorializing" material into memory storage is important to success in central nervous system processing of information, including reading. Neimark indicated that two classes of preliminary transformation are

performed upon incoming information (including written
language) at the early stages of thought—*analyzing* and
memorializing. The *analytic* transformation has to do with
focusing on properties and relations in the task situation;
it implies selective attention. *Memorializing* refers to procedures for coding material into memory storage to be
retrieved for later utilization. Neimark indicated that these
transformation processes plus a third factor of age possess
an ontogeny which is characteristic of all humans, and
proceed in an invariant sequence. In fact Neimark considered that the changes in the nature of preliminary
transformation of information underlie the cognitive developmental stages of Piaget's genetic epistemology. Neimark stressed that there is evidence demonstrating the in-
efficiency of incidental learning relative to intentional learning, and that the latter indeed requires specific skills
that are developed with time. The young child seems to
confuse recognition with recall or perhaps, as Neimark suggested, perception with memorization. Six-year-olds do not
organize material well and seem unaware that memorizing
requires extra efforts and the use of special cognitive
techniques. To six-year-olds all learning seems incidental.
Changes from a preoperational level to a concrete operations level of cognition have generally been explained by
invoking some sort of analytic mechanism, such as the ability to attend to both of two simultaneously varying properties. For example, given two identical balls of clay, the
preoperational child will say, after one of the balls has
been flattened, that there is now more (or less) clay in the
pancake than in the ball. Neimark argued that considera-
ations of logic in thinking need not arise in a child who
has not carried over stored information about the prior
state in the first place. Older children store information
by organization, repetition, and memorialization. College
students, who are responsible for ever greater volumes of
information, find that rote techniques of memorization do
not suffice and are constantly inventing new organizing

mnemonics and problem-solving heuristic methods for chunking information.

Neimark stressed the maturational or age-related factor and the differences between analytic and memorializing transformations by mentioning data which support the fact that form discrimination has been trained as early as eighteen months, whereas accurate drawing of simple forms such as squares and triangles is not attained much before age five. Production talents, as opposed to those which only ask for recognition, require in addition that one has stored information about defining properties and their relations for later retrieval to direct production.

Reading for meaning rather than just
reading words or sentences; reading
dynamics (success); contradictory evidence

Perhaps the most current vogue that purports to allow readers to quickly survey large amounts of written material in a comprehensible manner is the method of Reading Dynamics developed and advocated by Evelyn Wood. Wood (1969) stressed that words are signals which call forth a response in the "deep-well storage-banks of the mind;" but words that stand alone may be interpreted incompletely or erroneously. Only through viewing quickly large "word meaning groups" does comprehension become more accurate and complete. If the program which consists of 21 hours of instruction is followed, average reading rates of 250 words per minute may be increased by 3-6 times with good recall and comprehension. Using the datum that the words of even an overlearned phrase cannot be pronounced in less than 100 milliseconds apiece (600 words per minute), Neisser noted that since many people read faster than 300 or even 600 words per minute, they surely do not identify every word.

The usual explanation for this kind of reading relies on the concept of the redundancy of language, since it is known that readers and listeners can "fill in" as many as fifty percent of missing letters and words in English. This ability to supplement may be due to contextual clues or to information based on past experience. But to Neisser, such an account of reading for meaning was inadequate. There might be a plausible analogy between reading sentences without attending to specific words and recognizing words without attending to specific leters. In both word recognition and letter recognition the end product is a *name*, a structured verbal pattern in inner or outer speech. In successful rapid reading, the end product is not a bit of verbal behavior, but a *deep cognitive structure*. In rapid reading we attain a meaning without identifying individual words and we continuously take account of *new* constellations of words to construct *novel* thought processes (productivity of language?). Neisser summed up by indicating that reading is externally guided thinking and that the process is poorly understood. He added that however dubious we may be about the claims of reading improvement courses, we cannot refute them. Rapid reading for meaning cannot be explained within the framework of visual synthesis and verbal memory. We may not understand reading until we understand thought itself.

Graf (1973) questioned the claim that speed-readers absorb as much meaning from their material as they did when they read slowly, suggesting that the speed-reading courses taught skimming, not reading. The experiment, carried out with appropriate control groups, used four different types of literature—heavy fiction, light fiction, light nonfiction and heavy nonfiction. On the average reading speed in the experimental group was increased 221 percent, but comprehension suffered markedly in 51 of the 62 subjects. The group's average score for comprehension before the speed-reading course had been 66.1 percent; it was now 40.6 percent. Five of the 62 subjects, however, showed an increase in comprehension which correlated slightly with their higher grade-point average. Tests for comprehension were fill-in and multiple choice questions, the kinds of methods used by teachers of speed-reading courses to test their students. Graf summarized that comprehension is indeed a complex phenomenon.

The psycholinguistic interpretation of the
writing-reading process: the psychological
reality of phonological differences;
transformational rules apply to writing-reading
as well as to spoken language

It is on the comprehension aspects of the reading process that psycholinguistic theory and input have had great impact in recent years. Stressing the need to better understand the relation of syntax to meaning, Fleming (1969) observed that the more we know about the nature of language, its acquisition, use, and users, especially from the point of view of a transformational-generative grammar in which the speaker-listener, writer-reader *actively* participates, the more we shall be able to understand reading. Taking into account Bernstein's sociolinguistic concepts of elaborated and restricted codes in language resulting in real psychological differences, Shuy (1969) discussed differences in phonological and grammatical systems between standard English and inner-city Black English. Stressing that the differences are not overwhelming, Shuy noted that those who speak different dialects do understand one another. Yet significant contrasts exist, especially when one compares the verb systems of lower- and working-class Blacks with those of middle-class Blacks and with whites of all classes, particularly in the use of the copula and the auxiliary. Phonological and grammatical differences noted by frequency distribution studies pertain to multiple negation, *r* deletion, *l* deletion, consonant cluster reduction, and devoicing of word final consonants. The significance of the above differences as these youngsters begin to receive reading instruction, whether of a phonics or of a sight-see approach, should be taken into account. A startling example of a phonological confusion that might have had significant effects in psychological reality was cited by Crawford (1972). A question on a standardized IQ test was, "How many ears do you have?" The unhesitating reply was "fifteen." The examiner observed that the young man who was being tested had a Spanish surname and was about fifteen years old. What the young man had heard was "How many years do you have?" which is directly translated from the Spanish, "Cuantos años tiene Usted?"

Bormuth (1969) indicated that comprehension ability refers to a set of generalized knowledge-acquisition skills which permits a reader to acquire and exhibit information gained as a consequence of reading written language. Bormuth, speaking from the point of view of a psycholinguistic approach to reading, indicated that there are distinctions, if subtle ones, between comprehension and achievement testing. Achievement scores represent *how much of the knowledge in a specific passage* the student has been able to acquire. Comprehension scores represent *how well the student is able to acquire knowledge from written language of the type represented by that same passage.* The comprehension score involves an ability to *generalize* the student's performance on the tests which could be made from a population of passages. The distinction between achievement and comprehension is analogous to that between performance and competence in language. Bormuth indicated that designing an adequate comprehension task requires reassessments of theories and definitions, specifically about comprehension; he lamented that because of the achievement-comprehension confusion, much of the past research in these areas is not interpretable.

A native speaker possesses extensive sentence knowledge (innate transformational rules) of his or her language, which is related to the comprehension process, and involves structural and semantic aspects (Ruddell, 1969). A native speaker-listener, writer-reader can distinguish grammatical from ungrammatical sentences, even those never before encountered, can identify and understand ambiguous sentences with identical surface structures, such as "they are frying chickens," and can understand sentences with similar meaning but possessing different surface structures—"the boy ate the apple", versus "the apple was eaten by the boy." A native speaker-listener, writer-reader can generate and comprehend almost limitless numbers of novel utterances and sentences, suggesting an underlying rule governing competency. Ruddell reviewed data of several investigators which support the view that heard perceptual units correspond well to sentence constituent units (phrase structure) and therefore are psychologically real (Fodor and Bever, 1965). Ruddell mentioned the work of Ammon, who showed that both third-grade and adult subjects require more time to process and respond to information that occurs across phrase boundaries than to process and respond to that occurring within phrases. Ruddell, using the concepts of transformational grammar, suggested that sentences are processed from the surface structure level to an underlying or deep level for comprehension purposes. This deep structure is realized through transformational and rewrite rules and is integrated with a semantic component to convey meaning. Wardhaugh (1969) stressed that there is *active participation* by the speaker-listener, writer-reader, and submitted the following examples of sentences to be processed:

1. The man stole the car.
2. The car was stolen.
3. Who stole the car?

The first sentence demands that the reader understand that *the man* is the subject, the deep subject, of the sentence in which *stole the car* is the predicate, and *the car* is the deep object. The second sentence has a surface subject, *the car*; but the real subject, the deep subject, is an unspecified *SOMEONE*. *The car* is actually what was stolen, so *SOMEONE* stole it and *the car* is still the deep object. The deep structure accounts for the fact that a correct interpretation of *The car was stolen* requires an understanding that an unspecified person did the stealing and that this person stole the car. Sentence three is a question about *SOMEONE* who stole the car and seeks the identity of that *SOMEONE*.

Wardhaugh stressed that in teaching comprehension one must understand exactly what must be comprehended. It is not just words but rather *what must be comprehended*, that must be accounted for by a knowledge of the phonologic-syntactic-semantic relationships in a spoken or written sentence. The surface and deep (semantic) structures may relate to short- or long-term memory components of language processing. Ruddell quoted the work of Mehler, who showed that after subjects had been asked to memorize a series of complex sentences varying in grammatical type they tended to recall the sentences but in a simpler grammatical form. For example, a sentence in the passive was often recalled in its active form. A recoding of the sentence had occurred, maintaining the semantic content. It would appear that limited short-term memory deals with the less complex surface structures of sentences, while long-term memory deals with the more involved deep structures of a sentence, the latter relating to comprehension.

Successful reading is really reading for
meaning; studies with bilinguals

The relation and importance of meaning to successful reading has been investigated by Kolers (1973). In normal reading, such words as "was" and "saw" are rarely confused because only one of them will make sense in most contexts. Kolers maintained that this is true even to the point that both words could be eliminated from most texts with minimal effect on intelligibility. If one is reading for meaning, and not just enunciating aloud for a class, Kolers held that few readers will mistake "dog" for "bog," or "pig" for "dig," because the dissimilarity of meaning far exceeds the visual similarity of the members of such word pairs. Kolers argued that the skilled reader operates less at the level of words than at a semantic or logical level and that he may even disregard, in a sense, the printed text. Kolers described two interesting studies with French-English bilinguals to stress his point, namely, that a person who knows the language from which words are being flashed sees the concepts the words represent, not merely the words. Kolers first cited data from Waugh, which showed that the likelihood of recalling unrelated words, flashed at the rate of one per second, increases with the recurrence of any one word in the list. A word presented four times is twice as likely to be recalled as one that was presented only twice. The French-English bilinguals were presented with long lists of words, some appearing in French only, some in English only, and some as translated pairs such as "wheat - blé" and "snow - neige." Although presentation was haphazard the results clearly showed that the recall of a word in one language was aided by presenting its translation. The probability of recalling either "neige" or "snow" was equal to the probability of recalling "desk" and (repeated) "desk," and less than the probability of recalling "hat" or "shoe." In another study the ability of bilingual subjects to understand passages in which the two languages were mixed was compared to their understanding of similar passages in French only, or in English only. In the same allowed time the bilingual subjects were able to understand the mixed passages as well as they could understand the unilingual ones. Such would not have been the case, Kolers reasoned, if the readers had had to make all of the words of a mixed passage conform to a single language before they could understand them. Identifying unfamiliar words or reading proof is at a different level of the hierarchy of skills available to the competent reader, who usually treats words as symbols and operates on them in terms of their meanings and their relations to other symbols.

Successful reading relates to flexibility
of cognitive strategies

Gibson and her group stressed that graphic symbols must be perceptually interpreted in an invariant manner as a prerequisite to successful reading. Ruddell (1969), however, contended that success in reading has more to do with cognitive strategies, which are not rigid but versatile. As one is involved in writing-reading processes there is a constant need to obtain meaning. Ruddell presented data from a concept formation study of school children which showed that achieving readers were superior to nonachievers in flexibility, in that the achievers were better able to draw inferences from relevant clues and were better able to shift cognitive strategies when new standards were introduced. An important dimension in comprehending language consists in modifying and reorganizing a previously formed concept.

Piagetian cognitive development and its relation to writing-reading; egocentricity interferes with learning to read the words and comprehend the thoughts of others

It is unnerving to recognize that writing-reading instructions have not until very recently been related to Piagetian stages of cognitive development. Even the recent unique teaching-to-read approaches such as DISTAR (a method in which letters are named and pronounced in quick succession in an attempt to form the word), WORDS IN COLOR, and the ITA are still based on coding effectiveness and associative learning. As a result of these approaches children become successful word-callers but comprehension scores are falling (Arnolt, 1975).

Piagetian cognitive stages are not merely descriptive and sequential; they indicate that children think qualitatively differently from adults. Certain characteristics of the preoperational stage (ages two to seven years) impede learning of the English alphabet and its phonemic representations. The preoperational child manifests egocentrism. Because of this type of thinking the child believes that all people think as he does. Before the child can assimilate and accommodate the egocentric thoughts of his peers, he or she may not be particularly interested in learning to read words and thoughts of others.

Preoperational child has difficulty with
transformations (cognitive-perceptual); the
child tends to "center;" decentration appears
to be crucial to reading comprehension

Children at this stage manifest inability to follow transformations. Thought is not liberated from perceptions, for example, if a pencil has fallen from the table to the floor unwitnessed by the child, he cannot visualize the pencil *in flight* from the table to the floor. In teaching reading, individual grapheme-phoneme matches such as C, A, T can be taught to the very young. But letters which are transformed by their surroundings (C,A,T combined) denote a different graphemic-phonemic relationship. The separate sounds for the letters c/a/t do not sound like *cat* even if you "say them fast," as in the DISTAR method. The preoperational child, who has difficulty in analyzing the transformed words, would also have difficulty in sounding out the "a" of *mat, mate, mart, meat.*

A similar problem with the "a" sound would occur in *great, grate,* and *eight.* Piaget stressed that rather than memorize, children need to have a large conceptual base acquired from their own experience before words will have meaning. At this stage thought is largely intuitive in the sense that cognition is guided by perception (that which appears to exist) rather than by what adults would term "rational considerations." This is noted most vividly in the child's tendency to "center" on one particular static feature of the environment at a time.

The child focuses on *states* rather than on *transformations*, and focuses on only one such state at one time. He may "decenter" and focus on another state, but there is no logical connection in his mind between the two centerings and he does not focus on spatial relationships.

The centering child may have difficulty in concurrently learning and applying rules although he may have originally memorized the rule with ease. He cannot center on two or more thought processes at once. Thus it is difficult for the preoperational child to 1) name the grapheme-phoneme relationship, 2) (at the same time) put the letters together to form words, and 3) (at the same time) put words together to form sentences with meaning. The results are low comprehension scores in reading. Decentration therefore appears to be crucial to successful reading comprehension.

Reversibility of cognitive processes necessary to establish grapheme-phoneme, phoneme-grapheme matching

Reversibility of thought processes allows the child to perform the mental activities of following an operation from its conclusion back to its beginning and vice versa. The preoperational child, who is still at a stage of irreversibility, may find it difficult to convert graphemes to phonemes by memorization, as in reading, and then to validate his "knowledge" by reversing and attaching the right grapheme to a phoneme, as in writing. Until this ability to reverse develops, implying the existence of a state of cognitive flexibility and versatility as discussed by Ruddell, the child's perceptions of the world proceed like a series of projected lantern slides. There may be constant revision but there is no recording of these revisions. Because the foundation of thought is constantly shifting, the thinking of the preoperational child is characterized by instability and lack of organization. Hence the fleeting grasp of concepts these children often display (Weikart et al.,

1971). With this in view it is perhaps easier to understand how, if one presents a preoperational child with upper case letters, lower case letters, different type faces, manuscript and cursive writing, and variations in phoneme-grapheme matches, he or she might fail to read. This might be so until the cognitive processes of empathy (as opposed to egocentrism), ability to follow transformaticns, decentering, and reversibility develop, allowing the child to approach the stage of concrete operations, so that he or she might be better able to deal with transformed letters, and hold in mind rules of relationships while synthesizing meaning.

Cognitively oriented curriculum; emphasis on
process of learning; attention paid to child's
development level; internalization of words
versus memorization

A curriculum that is cognitively oriented is focused more on the *process* of learning than on facts or subject matter. Particular attention is paid to the individual child's developmental level. Piagetian theory advocates an activity-centered curriculum with many concrete experiences as well as social interactions with other children. Words should surround children for internalization rather than for memorization. The preoperational child should have the opportunity to build a perceptual and meaning base from his environment. This environment should emphasize interaction with concrete materials as well as pictorial and symbolic representations of reality. Exploration and manipulation are the key modes of experiencing; reading and books are part of the general environment. Learning to read and write becomes an extension of a child's own language and experience.

Temporal relation between symbolic
representation and language referent

It is always interesting to speculate about which occurs first, symbolic representations or the language referents for them. Brislawn (1975) investigated this area by studying the development of the concept of space. His findings indicated that both accurate perceptions of space relations and the prepositions used to describe those perceptions increase with age. Vertical space relations are learned earlier than those relating to horizontal dimensions. Static relations are learned at an earlier age than rotated ones, but accurate prepositional descriptions of space, both static and rotated, occur *after* the acquisition of operational structures representing those space relationships.

Assessment of reading readiness by stages of
cognitive development; individual cognitive styles

Arnolt suggested that several principal factors enter into the assessment of a child's readiness for formal reading instruction. First, the child's general level of cognitive development should be evaluated by testing procedures which are commercially available. One must attempt to determine the child's level of representing reality. Does he or she understand pictorial representations? Does he or she possess language concepts of words to be presented? According to Brislawn it would be inappropriate to present words such as "below" and "above," or "behind" and "in front of" before these spatial concepts are in the child's cognitive repertoire. Arnolt also suggested that it would be wise to find the child's major "mode of learning," for example, is the child essentially a visual, aural, or kinesthetic learner. This implies that even within the framework of normal cognitive development certain learning preferences or styles are inherent. The curriculum that is cognitively oriented is specifically designed to enable children to produce meaningful mental representations and so derive relations among objects and events, both real and represented, by especially stressing four content areas—classification, seriation, temporal, and spatial relations (Weikart et al, 1971).

Subareas in language functioning:
reading readiness tests; the ITPA, pros and cons

While the need for early and progressive reading achievement is recognized, there are many controversies about the predictability of reading success or failure. Assessing the many available reading readiness tests, Calfee and Venezky (1969) stressed that the component skills required for the reading process have not yet been well sorted out and that although performance on readiness subtests has been proposed as a source of diagnostic information, there is no clear evidence that results of such tests can predict success or failure in reading. Nor, they argued, is it apparent what remedial action should be taken when a child performs poorly on a readiness test, even on such a test as the Illinois Test of Psycholinguistic Abilities (ITPA), which is based on an elaborate model of language functioning. Calfee and Venezky contended that there is no consistent evidence that the ITPA can assess the systematic development of specific skills with age; they held that the ITPA tests a single talent, best described as "general linguistic ability."

In discussing the positive contributions of the ITPA Lamb (1969) indicated that language processing is composed of numerous tasks involving *several modes* of reception and expression, including the more complicated tasks of integration, storage, and retrieval. He stressed that the ITPA was designed as an *initial* diagnostic tool, and that the tester should maintain an overview. The ITPA is standardized for children from ages two-and-one-half to nine years. It originally included nine subtests; three were added later. The first six subtests have to do with representational levels, or the ability to mediate activities dealing with the meaning of linguistic symbols. Three psycholinguistic processes are involved. Two are decoding processes. These relate to the ability to obtain meaning from incoming linguistic symbols, that is, receptive language ability, as tested a) by auditory decoding (*Do airplanes fly?*), and b) by visual decoding (*See this. Now find one here.*) Two are association processes. These relate to the ability to meaningfully manipulate linguistic symbols internally, for example, inner language abilities as tested by auditory vocal association (*Soup is hot. Ice cream is* ___.), and by visual motor association (*Which one of these* [*star, glove, rose*] *goes with this* [*hand*]?). Two are encoding processes, the ability to express one's meaning fully by means of linguistic symbols, that is, expressive language ability as tested by verbal expression, or the ability to describe simple objects in several unique and meaningful ways, and manual expression, or the ability to express ideas through gestures (*Show me what you would do with this* [*pencil sharpener*]). The subtest of *grammatic closure* examines the subject's ability to use grammar and syntax naturally when one speaks (*Here is a man. Here are two* ___.). *Visual closure* pertains to the ability to identify a common object from a portion of the whole object. *Auditory vocal sequencing* measures the ability to produce a sequence of auditory stimuli from memory. The *visual motor sequencing* subtest examines the subject's ability to reproduce from memory a sequence of visually presented material. *Auditory closure* is the ability to fill in missing sounds to produce a complete word. *Sound blending* is the ability to put together and produce an integrated whole.

Characteristic profiles were obtained by the ITPA for certain clinically identifiable groups—normal, trainable mentally retarded, educable mentally retarded, cerebral palsied, deaf, receptive aphasics, and those with reading disabilities. The ITPA renders information about strengths and weaknesses in the subareas of language functioning and often can show whether the subject is a visual or auditory learner or both, indicating the best teaching modality for that child.

IV

Dysfunctions of Writing and Reading Language

Predicting reading failure—ten tests which form the basis for a successful predictive index for reading failure; studies of reading problems in prematures

The most impressive study for predicting reading failure has been that of De Hirsch, Jansky, and Langford (1966), who demonstrated that valid predictions of reading, writing, and spelling achievement can be made by evaluating children's perceptual-motor and language behavior at early ages. The authors stressed that children mature physiologically and psychologically along foreseeable lines, and that those children who lag severely in overall maturation can be predicted to fail academically. The overwhelming majority of children who suffer from spoken language disorders later also present difficulties with decoding and encoding printed and written language. Deviations in perceptuomotor organization are often concomitant with disturbances of spoken language. Lack of serviceable communicative tools hampers developing ego functions and secondary psychological problems of poor self-image often result.

Because of the great difficulties in which academically failing children find themselves De Hirsch and her associates attempted to determine whether a distinct identifiable pattern of perceptuomotor and language deficits at kindergarten age is *predictive* of difficulties with reading, writing, and spelling in subsequent years. They studied thirty boys and twenty-three girls, of whom forty percent were black. At the time of kindergarten testing, the median age of the fifty-three children was five years and ten months. All of the subjects were of lower middle-class backgrounds; all had been born at full term. Their IQs (Stanford-Binet) ranged from 84-116, none presented a significant sensory defect, and none showed evidence of psychopathology. The authors considered thirty-seven kindergarten-level tests which reflected the investigators' theoretical position, derived from the work of Piaget, Gesell, Werner, and Vygotsky, each of whom postulated evolving stages of sensorimotor, perceptual, and linguistic functioning. The testing involved four visits over a period of three years. De Hirsch and her colleagues developed a battery of ten tests selected from the original thirty-seven, each of which in their opinion contributed to the effectiveness of a successful predictive index of reading failure as a whole. These interestingly enough included tests that assessed many skills—cognitive, linguistic, and motor perceptual—again suggesting that many component skills are needed in reading. The tests were:

1. Pencil use
2. Bender Visual Motor Gestalt Test
3. Wepman Auditory Discrimination Test
4. Number of words used in a story
5. Categories. The child is asked to produce a generic name for each of a series of three word clusters (Tom-Bill-Jim = boys). Successful response reflects the beginnings of generalization.
6. Horst Reversals Test. The child is asked to visually match two- and three-letter sequences

which are presented both in correct and in reversed orders in a model.

7. Gates Word Matching Subtest. The child is asked to draw a line between the words that look the same.
8. Gates Word Recognition I. The child is asked to point to known words on index cards serially presented.
9. Gates Word Recognition II. The child is asked to point to known words on index cards spread on a table.
10. Gates Word Reproduction Test. The child is required to write from memory a known word.

De Hirsch et al. commented that the literature on the subject of prematurity presents contradictory findings, exemplifying the polarities of the nature-nurture dichotomy. Some investigators maintain that at kindergarten age prematurely born children measure up to those born at term, provided that their IQs fall within an average range, that gross neurological disorders are absent, and that a rich environment has been provided. Many others have commented on the high frequency of reading disabilities in the prematurely born. De Hirsch and co-workers compared fifty-three prematurely born subjects whose birth weights had ranged from two pounds and three ounces to four pounds and fifteen ounces, with the previously studied group of fifty-three children, all of whom had been born at term. Slight differences in sex and race favored the prematurely born. This group contained more girls, who are believed to be more mature than boys of the same age, and more white children, who are believed to enjoy more cultural advantages than their black peers. The prematurely born children showed poorer performances on thirty-six of the thirty-seven kindergarten tests; on fifteen of the tests differences in favor of the maturely born reached statistical significance. In addition, while the prematurely born showed some signs of "catching up" in some areas between the ages of five-and-one-half and eight years, their academic performance at the end of the second grade continued to lag. The investigators' findings in general were consistent with those of others who have observed a high incidence of academic failure and specific learning deficits among prematures of adequate intelligence.

Reading incompetence

Rates in relation to sex, ethnic group, geographic
locality, socioeconomic bracket, IQ, and
perinatal factors

Lack of competence in writing and reading can lead to disaster for an individual in a society many of whose intricacies and successes are based upon graphic symbol interpretation. Employability is increasingly contingent upon literacy. Those who cannot read today are to be the disadvantaged of tomorrow. They may well be impoverished economically and emotionally, and their misfortunes may be felt in various ways by their families and by the society in which they live. The ability to read makes available to men direct contacts with great minds of all times, opens vistas of sensitivity and understanding, and frees men from the rigidities and limitations of their own personal experience (Eisenberg, 1966). Yet in 1956 half of the world's adults were fully illiterate and only about one-third were functionally literate by the criterion of a fourth-grade reading level. By that standard in 1956, eleven percent of United States citizens could not read, the proportions varying by states from three and nine-tenths percent to twenty-eight and seven-tenths percent. Statistics with relation to the existence of *reading incompetence* based on the conventional definition as reading two or more grades below expected grade level vary from ten percent of children before they reach the seventh grade (Rabinovitch, 1968) to twenty to thirty percent of today's school children (Saunders, 1962). Generally, but with community-to-community variability, these data refer to "normals" and specifically exclude those children in more or less definable categories who are in specific treatment and educational programs such as the trainable mentally retarded, the educable mentally retarded, the multiply handicapped, the physically handicapped, the blind, the deaf, the aphasic, and those children described as autistic and primarily emotionally disturbed. Some of the children with reading incompetence do find themselves in classes for the educationally handicapped, neurologically handicapped, or learning disabled. Eisenberg (1966) supervised an epidemiological study which compared reading performances of urban and suburban groups and found that twenty-eight percent of sixth-grade children of the urban group were reading two or more years below grade level. Focusing attention specifically on the percentage of children more than one year below expected grade level in reading, the urban area had failure rates three times those of the suburban, and more than fifty times those of the private schools in the area. In a special study in which "reading incompetence" was defined as reading ability one year below grade level, such incompetence was found in nineteen and five tenths percent of boys; this percentage was more than twice as high as that for girls (nine percent), a finding substantiated by other studies and clinical experience. One geographic area allowed computation by race. Whereas twelve percent of white children were two or more years retarded in reading, the corresponding figure for black children was thirty-six percent. Interestingly, in a special study within each ethnic group, the male rate remained significantly higher than the female rate, sixteen and eight-tenths percent to seven and one-tenth percent for whites and forty-two percent to twenty-six percent for blacks. In a community of blacks and whites in which comparative data could be gathered, it is significant that seven percent of the white families, but sixty-two percent of the black families fell into the lowest socioeconomic class.

It is not the purpose of this book to deal specifically with the concept of IQ and its many attendant controversies. Yet Eisenberg noted that at least this argument should be stated—group IQ testing requires reading for its comprehension and success with both the IQ test and the reading test is a function of the total educational experience of the child. Therefore the fact that the median IQ for the urban group was about ninety-five, not the theoretically expected one hundred, does not really explain their much lower reading scores. Eisenberg admitted that not all intelligence development is experience-related, but that such development is affected to the extent that slum-dwellers of the urban subgroup suffer a heavier than usual burden of central nervous system injury stemming from social class-related complications of prenatal, natal, and early postnatal phase. Eisenberg suggested that herein we encounter a true biological difference, but that this difference is of far less magnitude than would appear from the statistics on reading incompetence.

Causes and definitions: secondary reading
incompetence, primary reading incompetence
(primary developmental dyslexia)

Basically most clinicians and investigators in many relevant disciplines agree that there are two groups of reading incompetents: 1) those in whom the reading incompetence is *secondary* or reactive to other pathologic states or abnormalities, and 2) those in whom the reading incompetency is of a *primary* nature, in that there is no evidence of definitive brain damage as determined by history or by physical and neurological examinations. Such primary reading incompetence has been termed (*primary*) *developmental dyslexia* (Saunders, 1962; Eisenberg, 1966; Rabinovitch, 1968; Gofman, 1969; Critchley, 1970b).

Difficulties with definition: overlapping
diagnostic categories lead to confusion; "soft
signs?" versus soft signs; interplay of
attentional and cognitive mechanisms

The rigidity of the definition, "no evidence of definitive brain damage," and the recently developing concept
of "soft signs" noted on neurological examination in some
children with learning disabilities have created confusion
and even doubts of the existence of the diagnosis of
primary developmental dyslexia. Terms such as "minimal
brain dysfunction" have come to the fore to take up the
slack in definition, and conceptual polarities have developed, ranging from Buchanan's statement (as cited by
Barlow, 1974) that "there are no soft signs, only soft
neurologists," to the notion of a continuum of psycho-
biologic development along which each of us is placed at
different and varying levels of talents and weaknesses. A
more hopeful term and one that is not unrealistic
especially in view of our growing understanding of cerebral hemispheric specialization (Ornstein, 1972; Galin and
Ornstein, 1972), would be *differential brain function*,"
rather than *minimal brain dysfunction*. Interpretations
of "neurological behavior" may vary according to the time
and place of observation. The observer's ability to describe
or measure behavior differs depending upon whether the
observations are made in the examining room or in the
classroom. A description of the subject's "true" neurological status (the total action-interaction of the subject
with his or her environment) should take into account the
subject's functioning in a classroom of thirty peers with
all of its attendant distractions—sights, noises, touches—
and with existing and expected fears and joys. In recognition of the need to take these factors into consideration,
some auditory discrimination tasks have recently been re-
standardized so that assessment can be obtained with
and without background noise. Sensitive observers, when

giving standardized IQ and reading tests to distractible-hyperactive youngsters, occasionally relax time rules and divide the tests into various time periods, so that problems with attentional mechanisms will not be interpreted as cognitive difficulties. In some situations standardized tests have been given when a distractible-hyperactive youngster has taken an appropriate central nervous system stimulant, so that he is enabled to sit still long enough to finish the test.

In a well-designed study Adams et al (1974) assessed the existence of soft neurological signs in a group of youngsters with learning disabilities, including some with primary developmental dyslexia, and an appropriate control group, and found that except for significantly depressed diadochokinesis (ability to perform rapidly alternating hand movements) and graphesthesia (the sense by which figures or letters written on the skin are recognized) in the learning-disabled group, none of the other soft signs (eye-hand preference, balance, stereognosis [the faculty of perceiving and understanding the form and nature of objects by the sense of touch], hand-finger immobility, finger localization) could distinguish the two groups.

The choreiform syndrome (ceaseless, rapid, complex, involuntary muscle movements). Previously Prechtl (1962) had written about the choreiform syndrome, and Ayres (1972) about difficulties with sensory-integrative functioning. Like Adams, however, they did not limit their observations of these relatively specific problems to dyslexics, thus creating overlapping diagnostic categories, but observed them in children with learning disabilities in general. Prechtl considered that the children with the choreiform syndrome were a distinct group but that the group might overlap clinically with dyslexic youngsters, because difficulties in fixating and in concentration (because of the choreiform activity) were common to the two groups. To exemplify the spectrum of possibilities Prechtl indicated that he and his colleagues had found several children with a severe form of the choreiform syndrome, with IQs of over 130 and with no learning difficulties per se. Prechtl suggested that the high IQ had enabled those youngsters to compensate for their neuromuscular problems.

Sensory integrative dysfunctioning. Ayres has written about dysfunctions of sensory integration in learning disabilities in general, and has discussed disorders of postural and bilateral integration, developmental apraxia, tactile defensiveness, and all manner of difficulties with form and space perception (part-whole discrimination, figure-ground discrimination, left-right discrimination). Her diagnostic categories overlap at times with those of primary developmental dyslexia. It is perhaps because of lack of recognition and definition of the subgroups within the framework of the learning disabilities which are not mutually exclusive (language delays, motor-perceptual dysfunctions, dyslexias-dysgraphias, distractibility-hyperactivity syndromes) that confusion arises as to whether or not there are positive albeit "soft" signs found on neurological examination of those children and adults who have primary developmental dyslexia.

The need for refined studies and interdisciplinary collaboration. Barlow (1974) suggested that, in view of the controversy over "soft signs," the most reasonable way to proceed is to assess each child in trouble by means of a most refined and individualized neuropsychological study. This view is also held by Davison (1974), who further stressed that significant strides in this field will depend upon close collaboration between the medically trained neuroscientist (clinicoanatomical studies) and the psychologically trained clinical neuropsychologist (developing and validating comprehensive operational definitions).

Secondary reading incompetency

In secondary reading incompetency, two subdivisions have been recognized:

Due to "frank brain damage;" pitfalls of cause-and-effect thinking

The capacity to learn to read may be impaired by *"frank brain damage"* manifested by a clearcut neurological deficit. This state is similar to the suddenly occurring adult alexic syndromes, and is usually accompanied by other aphasic difficulties. In these patients a definite history of pre- or perinatal distress (marked prematurity, anoxia, or trauma) or of encephalitis or later cerebral trauma is obtained. Nevertheless relationships that are presumed to be of cause and effect must be assessed carefully, not only because the assignment of cause may create guilt feelings in family members, but also in relation to medicolegal ramifications and the possibility of litigation. In the Learning Disabilities Clinic in the Department of Pediatrics of the Kaiser-Permanente Medical Center in Oakland, California, two of the two thousand patients seen were about eleven years old and had secondary reading incompetence with a definite history of recent head trauma—one had fallen from a second-story window, the other had suffered an automobile accident. Yet on careful examination of the past history obtained both from the parents and from the school, it was clear that problems with reading had been evident from age six years, some four years before the head trauma in each instance.

Due to sociopsychological disadvantages

The second group of patients with secondary reading incompetency includes those whose innate capacity to learn to read is intact, but because of certain secondary exogenous factors of a sociopsychological nature this capacity is insufficiently utilized to achieve a reading level commensurate with mental age. These factors include quantitative and qualitative defects in teaching, limitations in cognitive stimulation, chronic physical illness, and deficiencies in motivation stemming from individual psychopathology, socal disadvantages, and lack of opportunity, or all three. Certainly fatigue, anxiety, fear, hunger, depression, as well as states of diminished self-concept for any of a variety of reasons can interfere with the learning processes, to which reading is fundamental (Eisenberg, 1966; Rabinovitch, 1968).

Expectations and self-fulfilling prophecies

Lower expectations of achievement from disadvantaged youngsters may play significant roles in their future academic failures in the sense of self-fulfilling prophecies (Rosenthal and Jacobson, 1968). In studies of interpersonal expectations those children (the experimental group) from whom intellectual growth was expected (via contrived scores on a "test for intellectual blooming") gained intellectually but also were seen by their teachers as becoming more interesting, curious, and happy as their need for social approval lessened. But the slow-track children of the experimental group (of whom IQ gains were also expected) were not rated as favorably relative to their control group peers as were the children of the medium and fast tracks. In many subjects unfortunately a multiplicity of factors which result in a vicious cycle of organic-psychogenic interactions lead to academic failure.

Polyglotism: cause or not of secondary
reading incompetence?

Bilingualism (and its often attendant cofactor, frequent changes of home and school) has been cited as one of the possible exogenous causes of secondary reading incompetence. Yet Critchley (1968) doubted that this is an etiologic factor, citing as evidence several of his subjects who were true polyglots, the most outstanding of whom was a university lecturer's son who was dyslexic in Afrikaans, English, Gaelic, French, and Latin. Another of Critchley's subjects was a bilingual Anglo-Lebanese boy dyslexic in both English and Arabic, implying that the laterality of the language does not play an etiologic role. It was Critchley's contention that these were cases of primary developmental dyslexia manifesting itself in polyglots rather than examples of secondary reading incompetence. At the Learning Disabilities Clinic of the Department of Pediatrics, Kaiser-Permanente Medical Center, Oakland, California, there is a thirty-five-old adult subject who has had adequate educational opportunities and speaks Hungarian, Hebrew, English, and German well, yet is dyslexic and dysgraphic (has difficulty in placing thoughts in appropriate graphic forms including problems with spelling) in all four languages. In the same clinic there is a thirty-year-old Mexican-American who has attended school in both countries, speaks English by day at work and Spanish in the evening at home, and is dyslexic and dysgraphic in both languages. Nevertheless the picture is not totally clear, and Critchley (1970b) indicated the possibility that bilingualism, whether enforced or facultative, may constitute an added burden on "poor readers;" he cited the high incidence of "dyslexia" (twenty-two and five-tenths percent) noted by Chesni in Swiss subjects who were obligatory bilinguals in French and German.

Sociobiological cause for secondary reading
incompetence: malnutrition; malnourished infants
compared with adequately nourished in perceptual
and cognitive development; the vicious cycle of
biological and environmental handicapping

Malnutrition has biological as well as social effects, especially on the rapidly developing and therefore vulnerable central nervous system. In his review of this issue Wolman (1973) stated that malnutrition is the greatest single contributor to infant and child mortality in most of the developing countries of the world. When mothers are undernourished, fetal growth tends to slow during later pregnancy and the frequency of "small-for-date" babies is increased as a result. The perinatal morbidity and mortality rates for such infants are higher than for normal sized infants, and these small-for-date babies are prone to show lasting sublethal effects. Severe malnutrition in early infancy may cause physical and at times intellectual retardations. The lags in mental development in the malnourished are not restricted to motor components; in addition they affect problem-solving ability, language, personal-social development, general intelligence, intersensory integration, and perceptual-visual competence, the levels of which are significantly below those observed in adequately nourished siblings or matched controls.

Cravioto and Delicardie (1970) performed follow-up examinations for periods extending as long as ten years in severely malnourished infants and children who were hospitalized at the Hospital Infantil de Mexico in 1959, especially with relation to the development of specific cognitive functions (reading and writing). Birch and Belmont (1964) had shown that auditory-visual competence as a form of intersensory integration not only exhibited characteristic developmental patterns in normal school children, but could also be used as a measure to distinguish good from poor readers. Cravioto and Delicardie showed that when performance on an auditory-visual integration test by index patients with malnutrition was compared age for age with that of siblings, the malnourished children clearly scored well below their siblings. In a second study, visual-kinesthetic intersensory integration (an ability related to successful writing) was tested. Again, age by age, the children who had recovered from severe malnutrition showed significantly lower performance levels than their siblings. Testing for geometric form recognition yielded similar results in children aged five to nine years, but at age nine years the performance levels of the children who had recovered from severe malnutrition were similar to those of their siblings. On the Mexican form of the WISC, Full Scale, Verbal, and Performance scores were significantly lower in the previously severely malnourished children than in their siblings. Recognizing the time needed for hospitalization for the severely malnourished, Cravioto and Delicardie cautioned that the interference with cognitive functioning which results from early severe malnutrition may also reflect interference with experience and mothering. Whether the results of severe malnutrition are chemical, environmental, or both, the deleterious effects of handicapped skills in reading and writing diminish the affected person's ability to profit from educational experiences and render him prone to school failure and subnormal adaptive functioning. If that person later becomes a parent his poor socioeconomic environment may persist through another generation. He would tend to rear the children in conditions that would predispose the offspring to malnutrition.

Primary developmental dyslexia: definition;
still largely a diagnosis of exclusion;
diagnostic overlap with other components
of the minimal brain dysfunctions

This group comprises those subjects who are deficient in the ability to deal with letters and words as symbols, with resultant diminished ability to integrate the meaningfulness of written material. Although this concept is hotly contested the problem appears to reflect a basic disturbed pattern of neurologic organization. Most workers have held that this deficiency is endogenous, biologic, and perhaps genetic in etiology, with often profound secondary emotional problems. These *primary* reading incompetencies, *primary developmental dyslexia*, said to be present in about five to ten percent of the general population (Critchley, 1970b), are still to a great extent diagnosed by exclusion with the problems inherent in the exclusion process, in that the children with primary developmental dyslexia have no visual or hearing problems. Their general intellectual functioning is well within normal limits although they may show marked divergencies in responses to subtests, they have no *obvious* neurological deficit, they have no *primary* emotional disturbance, they have had *adequate* conventional educational opportunities, they were originally well motivated, they came from culturally adequate homes, and yet they cannot learn to read with normal proficiency (Eisenberg, 1966; Rabinovitch, 1968). Enhancing the complexity of the diagnostic problem is the fact that the syndrome of (primary developmental) dyslexia-dysgraphia often does not exist alone in children or adults, but may occur concomitantly with one or more of the three other major clinical entities within the framework of the minimal brain dysfunctions, such as the motor-perceptual dysfunction syndromes, the syndromes of distractibility, hyperactivity, and decreased attention span, and the syndromes of the language delays.

Historical methods of attempting to teach writing-reading: phonics methods, whole-word methods, kinesthetic methods

With the development of written language various methods have been suggested through the centuries to insure success in reading, writing, and spelling processes. An important stimulus to the generation of such varied systems has been the failures of some of those taught to succeed in acquiring these abilities. Fernald (1943) cited Quintilian, who in about A.D. 68, as a part of his plan for Roman education, advocated that the letters be taught first, then syllables, then words, and finally sentences. Before the Reformation the only materials available for reading were books pertaining to religious matters. From the fifteenth to the eighteenth century primers based on religious teachings were printed for children in which the text was accompanied by letters of the alphabet and various combinations of vowels and consonants. Fernald stated that in 1532 the first ABC book was printed in Germany in a rebus style in which a letter was connected to a picture; such as "A"—ape. This method has persisted to modern times. "Whole" word methods have been applied with varying success and failure since the seventeenth century. Horace Mann in 1840 criticized another approach, namely, the attempt to teach the child to read by having him spell the word by speaking the letters of which it is composed, for example, by spelling "law" aloud, in which the letters are pronounced "el, a, double ū." "Can we wonder," Mann asked, "that the progress of a child should be slow when we place such unnecessary impediments as these in his way?" Fernald reviewed the methods of learning to read by word-group which are currently in vogue; the origin of these methods may lie in earlier times when children repeated in concert the contents of books at which they were looking. However, questions arise regarding how children acquire the meanings of separate words if these words are always learned as part of a group. If the word is one that the child has already used with understanding in speech, then it already has meaning in a conceptual (Piagetian) sense; shades of meaning are added by the context of the material read. Fernald anticipated Kolers' (1973) observation that it is often possible to infer the meaning of a new word or to get a new meaning from an old word from the context of the total word group.

Fernald reviewed learning-to-read techniques indicating that every conceivable visual or phonetic, or visual-phonetic method has been tried in the past, but that in some children only kinesthetic methods seem to work. She cited historical data, developing the concept of a kinesthetic method. Plato stated that when a boy was not yet clever in writing the master should first draw lines, then give the boy the tablet and make him write as the lines direct. Horace spoke of coaxing children to learn their letters by tidbits of pastry made in the form of letters. Quintilian said that it was a mistake to teach children to repeat the alphabet before they know the form of the letters, which they could learn from tablets or blocks. As soon as the letters are recognized, they should be written. Fernald, in 1943, felt that in most of the schools the child was supposed to learn to read before he learned to write so that even this kinesthetic experience was denied him during the early learning process. Charlemagne learned to write by having engraved tablets made on which he traced with a stylus to guide his hand in following the outline of the characters. Robert Graves resented a caning he received at school especially because he was hit upon his hands—hands which he felt were unusually sensitive. Graves indicated that he lived much in his hands and that his visual imagery was defective, so that he memorized largely by the sense of touch. Fernald stated that if the kinesthetic method is to be used for the development of word recognition, the word form must be represented by the child's movements, especially those of his hands in contact with sand, sandpaper, or chalk-board, on which he employs tracing techniques.

Acquired language disorders; relation between alexia and aphasia; alexia and dyslexia

The current concept of a specific and constitutional type of difficulty in learning to interpret written symbols had its origin in experiences with acquired brain disease by a process of analogy (Critchley, 1970b). There is a relation between alexia and aphasia, but it is not clear cut. For almost as long as aphasia has been recognized awareness has existed that in some cases of speech loss there might also be a concomitant loss of the patient's capacity to attach meaning to printed or written symbols. Terms such as "alexia," "dyslexia," or "verbal amnesia" have been used conventionally for difficulties with the interpretation of graphic symbols. Generally *alexia* refers to acquired dysfunctions; *dyslexia* is specific to constitutional problems. Critchley (1970b) cited Kussmaul, who in 1877 proposed the term "word-blindness" for an isolated aphasic loss of the ability to read in persons whose powers of intellect, vision, and speech remain intact. Kussmaul recognized, however, that "word-blindness," like "word-deafness," seldom occurs as an isolated defect, usually being combined with other dysphasic symptoms such as loss of words of an amnestic nature, or with agraphia. Critchley, tracing the historical background of the subject, indicated that as increasing numbers of cases of acquired alexia were reported, two main groups of affected patients were noted. One group maintains the ability to write, while in the other, that ability is lost. But some alexic patients are still able to write even though they cannot read back what they have written. It was said of them that they write as though their eyes were shut. This latter group has been thought of as having "subcortical word-blindness;" those with alexia and agraphia as having "cortical word-blindness." Critchley stressed, however, that there are many incomplete and inconsistent symptom complexes, with corresponding problems in terminology. Critchley was critical of the term, "pure alexia," which implies *total* and *isolated* inability to read; he suggested that with further probing the investigator could discover other disorders in the realm of language in such patients and that total failure to interpret each written symbol is rarely found as an acquired deficit.

Aphasia as a disturbance of language; relations among spoken language, written language, and mutism; aphasiology as the study of central disorders of language with alexic variants

Geschwind (1971) stressed that aphasia is a disturbance of *language*, not simply of speech, and that if a person is totally mute one cannot be sure whether he is aphasic. Geschwind considered as a simple rule of thumb that in the patient with distorted speech output, if when that speech is transcribed it shows that the patient is producing correct English sentences, he is not suffering from aphasia but from some form of articulatory disability. If a patient is able to produce fully normal language in written form but does not speak, one can safely conclude that he is suffering not from aphasia but from mutism. Such a condition is often seen in patients with Parkinson's disease who have undergone bilateral thalamotomy. Interestingly, if speech returns in this condition, it may be severely dysarthric (characterized by imperfect articulation of speech) but the patient will not manifest difficulties in word-finding or in grammar.

Critchley (1970a), in the same line of thought, defined *aphasiology* as "the study of the phenomena of central disorders of language," and regarded alexia as that variant of aphasia in which the most conspicuous feature is an extreme difficulty in the interpretation of literal symbols by way of visual channels. Touching upon an area that had been emphasized by Fernald (1943), Critchley described alexic patients who are unable to interpret a letter or a word at sight, but who still can deduce its meaning by tracing kinesthetically the outlines of the symbol with a fingertip. A distinction should be made between the ability to read aloud with understanding of the text, and that of silent comprehension. In alexic patients ordinarily both performances are impaired but occasionally some measure of dissociation occurs, a dichotomy that is also noted in dyslexic-dysgraphic youngsters in the classroom.

Geschwind's description of Wernicke's aphasia: incomprehension of both spoken and written language

Two syndromes stand out prominently as disorders that are often characterized by inability to read (Geschwind, 1962). The more common of the two is Wernicke's aphasia, occurring with lesions of the posterior superior temporal region, in which the patient shows severe incomprehension of both spoken and written language together with a characteristic speech pattern. There is fluent speech (as opposed to nonfluent speech, associated with lesions of Broca's area), which is often totally incomprehensible as a result of the use of circumlocution, neologisms, and distorted or incorrect words. In Wernicke's aphasia there is also inability to write correctly.

Geschwind's description of Dejerine's patient
with pure word-blindness without agraphia, who
could identify letters by tracing contours; loss
of ability to interpret roman but not arabic
numerals; disconnection of the right visual cortex
from the left angular gyrus caused pure
word-blindness without agraphia (Dejerine); lesions
of the angular gyrus per se cause word blindness
with agraphia; Geschwind's speculation about
what Dejerine might have thought about the
cause of primary developmental dyslexia

A more restricted and less common syndrome is "pure word-blindness without agraphia." Although the existence of this syndrome is disputed by some authors, Geschwind was of the opinion not only that it indeed exists clinically, but also that it establishes a confirmed anatomical locus for a specific function. Geschwind cited Dejerine's report of a case, in 1892, as a masterpiece of neurological-clinico-pathological correlation. Dejerine's patient, an intelligent sixty-eight-year-old man, suddenly observed that he could no longer read a single word even though visual activity (except for right hemianopia [defective vision or blindness in half of a visual field]) was within normal limits, and he could speak fluently and understand all spoken speech. Writing, both spontaneous and to dictation, was correct, but the patient could not read what he had written. Surprisingly, and reminiscent of Fernald's observations in dyslexic children, Dejerine's patient could identify isolated letters by tracing their contours with his finger, or by allowing the examiner to move the patient's finger in the air. Later observers working with patients like Dejerine's have noted a remarkable discrepancy between loss of letters and preservation of numbers, in that the ability to read arabic numerals persisted while roman numerals seemed to present the same difficulties as the other letters. Interestingly Dejerine's patient, who had been a skilled musician, was now totally unable to comprehend musical notation. Four years later he died of a cerebral vascular accident. On post-mortem examination the older lesion (the cause of the pure word-blindness without agraphia) was found to be in the medial and inferior aspects of the left occipital lobe. Dejerine concluded that the ability to read depends upon connections going from the right occipital cortex across the corpus callosum to the left-sided language areas in the posterior temporal region, and that in his patient, because of the *extensive* destruction of white matter in the left occipital lobe, the connecting fibers to the right occipital cortex had most probably been destroyed. Dejerine believed that it was specifically the disconnection of the right visual cortex from the left angular gyrus which led to pure word-blindness without agraphia, but that lesions of the angular gyrus per se caused pure word-blindness with agraphia.

The preservation of "tactile" or "kinesthetic" reading in pure word-blindness without agraphia stands in contrast to its loss in pure word-blindness with agraphia. The latter syndrome is the result of a lesion of a cortical area which functions in an unknown manner in the operations done on visual language. Once the pertinent cortical area has been destroyed comprehension of written language is lost regardless of its mode of presentation. Yet, by a suitably placed lesion one can specifically disconnect from this cortical area the ability to comprehend visually presented material alone, while preserving the transmission of somesthetically presented stimuli. Geschwind speculated as to what Dejerine might have thought about congenital (constitutional) dyslexia; since the youthful central nervous system displays marked powers in finding alternative means of compensating for damage to localized areas, and since the angular gyrus acts in some specific way to process visual language, *bilateral* nondevelopment of this region would be the minimum substrate for difficulty in learning to read.

Clinico-anatomical study of loss of ability to read braille

Especially in view of clinico-anatomical data relating to localization of function in the central nervous system, it is perhaps appropriate to mention some unusual patients with disorders of nonarticulate speech. Critchley (1970a) cited a patient of Gloning et al., who at the age of twenty-two years was blinded, and who then learned to read braille fluently, using both index fingers either alone or in conjunction. At age fifty-eight years after a pneumonectomy for lung cancer the patient began to notice increasing clumsiness of the left hand and difficulty with braille reading. Although he could feel the dots, he could no longer interpret them, and he had difficulty in writing braille, both spontaneously and to dictation. Tactile interpretation of words was much harder than that of letters. He especially confused braille signs that were similar in form (*Q* and *ST*), or that were mirror opposites (*E* and *I*). At operation and later at autopsy metastatic growths were found in *both* the left and the right parietal areas, an especially significant combination of lesions for a blind person. It appears that the primary sensory field for reading for the blind is not the visual sphere, but the hand area within the postcentral convolution of the cerebral cortex. In the blind reading is transferred from the visual sphere into the tactile kinesthetic sphere. Critchley indicated that Gloning et al. believed that their patient had alexia for braille because of the bilateral parietal involvement.

Constitutional dyslexia including difficulties with Morse code

Critchley (1970a) described a young, intelligent naval cadet from a distinguished family who was referred for neuropsychiatric examination because of bizarre spelling errors and because of inability to learn Morse signaling. At school the subjects in which he had done most poorly were English and French; he had done well in chemistry and mathematics, especially geometry. His grammar was excellent, but he frequently made spelling errors, such as "Britian" for "Britain." Although he had originally memoorized the Morse alphabet in twenty minutes, he experienced great difficulty in sending, and especially in receiving Morse and also in flashing light signals, although he proved to be adept at semaphore and hoists of signal flags. He described his difficulty by saying that he was unable to distinguish between a dot and a dash, either by light flash or by buzzer. He also found it difficult to write large numbers which were dictated to him, such as 5,400,002. After careful analysis of all of this patient's disabilities Critchley concluded that the entire group could be regarded as aspects of a single defect. Difficulties in spelling, in writing down large figures, and in recognizing the component parts of a set of Morse symbols are instances of misspelling, whether of a series of letters, numerals, or dots and dashes. The difficulty in correctly putting on paper a number running into six or seven figures is really an instance of misspelled cyphering; it is not acalculia (inability to do simple arithmetical calculations). Similarly, the inability to gauge correctly the exact number of dashes or dots in a given set, or to differentiate between a dot and a dash, is analogous to misspelling in Morse. Since in addition the patient at one time did not recognize his own spelling errors when confronted with them, Critchley considered that this case was in the category of congenital dyslexia, a type of symbolic imperception with added difficulties in serial organization.

Primary developmental (constitutional)
dyslexia or acquired dyslexia (alexia)?
Possible overlapping of categories, for example,
congenital arteriovenous anomaly

Rabinovitch (1968) indicated that among his many dyslexic patients were some with several outstanding neurological deficits which made it difficult to determine whether the diagnosis should be constitutional dyslexia or acquired alexia. A patient who was followed from age nine to twenty-seven years had marked dyslexia as well as psychomotor and akinetic seizures. The EEG showed focal abnormality in the left parieto-occipital region. Skull roentgenograms indicated the presence of an abnormal vascular shadow in the temporoparietal area which led eventually to the diagnosis of a congenital anomaly of arteriovenous communication. In spite of intensive efforts to remediate the reading difficulty the patient remained completely illiterate. Among fifty children with severe reading incompetence (Rabinovitch, 1968), the hospital record or history showed that forty-six percent had either definite or suggestive evidence of brain damage, raising the question whether the remaining fifty-four percent had a hereditary (constitutional) type of primary developmental dyslexia, again bringing up all the pitfalls of a diagnosis of exclusion.

Perinatal distress factors in secondary reading incompetence; the biological continuum of "reproductive casualty"?

Kawi and Pasamanick (1958) suggested that in some children there is an association between the development of reading disorders and certain maternal and fetal factors. Birth records were obtained for 372 white boys born in Baltimore between 1935 and 1945. When those with reading disorders were compared with controls, significantly larger numbers were seen to have been born prematurely and to have shown abnormalities during the prenatal and perinatal periods. In addition sixteen and six-tenths percent of the boys with reading disabilities and only one and five-tenths percent of those without reading disorders had been exposed to maternal complications which included preeclampsia (a toxemia of late pregnancy), hypertensive disease, and bleeding during pregnancy, all of which, Kawi and Pasamanick believed, may lead to fetal anoxia. Knobloch and Pasamanick (1959) have developed a very organically based concept, that reading disorders of some children constitute "mild" components of the continuum of "reproductive casualty," the lethal components of which consist of abortions, stillbirths, and neonatal deaths, while its sublethal components might consist of cerebral palsy, epilepsy, or mental deficiency.

Congenital word-blindness and strephosymbolia

Although cases of developmental dyslexia were described as early as 1895 and 1896 in *The Lancet*, a definitive monograph entitled "Congenital Word Blindness" by James Hinshelwood, a Glasgow eye surgeon, appeared in 1917, ending a period of description and identification and starting one of analysis and discussion. The word "dyslexia" was first used by Professor Berlin of Stuttgart in describing an unusual case of word-blindness in 1887 (Critchley, 1970b). Orton (1925) described, among a series of children who had been designated by their teachers as "dull" or "subnormal," a high proportion whose chief difficulty was learning to read. Noticing that these children exhibited coexisting left-handedness or ambidexterity and a tendency towards reversals when they attempted to read or write, Orton created the term *strephosymbolia* to indicate that their problems of "mixed symbols" were due to "a failure to establish an exclusively unilateral (cerebral) dominance." His analysis of the abnormality indicated that confusion resulted from reversals in the memory images of symbols, causing "a failure of association between the visually presented symbol and its concept."

Geographic distribution of developmental dyslexia; Kana/Kanji differences

Critchley (1970b) stated that developmental dyslexia does not occur only in countries whose language contains "spelling illogicalities", such as English and Scandinavian, but also in countries where the written language is more strictly phonetic, as in Germany, Spain, Hungary, Romania, Czechoslovakia, Greece, and Italy. Makita (1968), however, stressed the rarity of reading problems among Japanese children. He implied that the cause was philological rather than psychological, in that English (in which most case reports appear) exceeds by far all other Western languages in the number of words containing irregular or unstable relations between spelling and pronunciation. Japanese Kana (syllabic script), however, stands in extreme contrast to English in this respect. In Kana, the syllable-phoneme relation is almost a key-to-keyhole situation. Critchley (1970a), however, drew attention to the fact that two scripts are used in Japan—Kana (syllabic) and Kanji (ideographic)—and attributed the overall rarity of dyslexia in Japan to statistical skewing resulting from the relative rarity of dyslexia in Kanji readers. Tending to corroborate Critchley's point, the few studied patients with dysgraphia among the Japanese have shown a tendency to be dyslexic in Kanji (Chinese characters) far less frequently than in the indigenous Kana script, probably, Critchley reasoned, because Kanji is much more concrete in nature than Kana.

Example of Chinese ideographic dysgraphia

Critchley (1970a) reported a fascinating case which may have important implications for left and right cerebral hemispheric functioning in the dyslexias and dysgraphias. A Chinese sea captain, literate and with hypertension, sustained transient right hemiparesis resulting three weeks later in dysgraphic mirror-reversal Chinese ideograms. Critchley concluded that Chinese ideographic dysgraphia may at times be due to a disorder of spatial thought rather than to an impairment of language. A constructional apraxia of parietal origin may render a Chinese patient unable to copy or to execute written material, even though there is no aphasia. The responsible lesion, Critchley believed, may be in the left or the right hemisphere. Critchley (1970a) presented another case of dysgraphia in a Chinese, which was caused by an astrocytic glioma of the left temporal lobe, in which problems with the ideograms included those that were missed completely, those that were replaced by incorrect ones, and those that were composed of incorrect strokes. Each of these difficulties indicated imperfect recognition and recall.

Processing differences in a "bilingual" Kana-Kanji
speaker-hearer, writer-reader; kinesthetic
activation of graphic-sound associations in Kana
(usually unsuccessful in Kanji); possible
relation to Boder's dyslexic subgroup

A recent report by Sasanuma (1974) implied that different neurophysiological mechanisms underlie the strategies for the retrieval of Kanji and Kana words, that these scripts represent different modes of linguistic behavior, and that in a "bilingual" Kanji-Kana reader-speaker the ability either to write or to read may be impaired independently of one another. Sasanuma reported a forty-three-year-old high-school teacher who suddenly had an attack of numbness affecting the right half of the body. A few moments later he could not read the newspaper. Assessment one month later showed serious reading impairment and mild difficulties in writing both Kanji and Kana, but all spoken language functions, such as the reception and production of spoken language, including spontaneous speech, repetition of sentences, and auditory comprehension, appeared to be intact. In contrast to the well-presented abilities to handle spoken language, the patient had marked problems with written language, especially in reading both Kanji and Kana.

The outstanding feature of the problem was that the patient used different strategies in handling the two types of written symbols. Both oral reading and oral com-

prehension were severely impaired except for four out
of twenty presented high-frequency words in Kanji. With
Kana he tried to pronounce each symbol, one after another,
sometimes using his finger to trace the outline of the
sign, usually in the air. When he finally succeeded in
vocalizing every syllable of the word (with much trial
and error) and obtained the sound shape of the word as
a whole, then he suddenly grasped the word's meaning.
The grapheme-meaning association was defective, but it
seems that the sound-meaning association remained intact.
Thus, to comprehend the meaning of a word in Kana, the
patient had to convert the visual pattern (graphic form)
of the word into its auditory pattern by pronouncing aloud
each constituent symbol. He could do this with time if he
was allowed to trace each Kana sign leading to the kinesthetic activation of graphic-sound associations. In general,
his comprehension of words written in Kanji took place
much faster than of those in Kana. This was probably due
to the use of *direct graph-meaning association*. When he
came across a difficult word, however, perhaps a Kanji
word not previously existing in his repertoire, this direct
approach did not work as well as it did in Kana. For instance, he had more trouble in converting the graphic form
into its sound pattern. If he did not immediately grasp the
Kanji meaning by *direct graph-meaning association*, he
would move his right index finger over and over to trace the
strokes of the Kanji characters as if trying to actuate the
association between the kinesthetic pattern of the word
and its sound pattern or its meaning, a behavior usually
not successful with the Kanji.

While there were only a few words written in Kana
which the patient could read at normal speed, if enough
time was allowed he could manage to decipher most of the
rest of them by means of a round-about graph-sound-mean-
ing strategy. On the other hand, there were many more
Kanji words for which the patient showed normal instan-

taneous comprehension; for example, he retained direct graph-meaning associations. The difference may be explained by the inherent difference in the mode of processing of the two types of symbols as a direct graphic approach for the Kanji via whole-word recognition and an indirect phonetic approach for the Kana. Another interesting aspect of this case was the tendency for confusions to occur between graphic symbols of similar configurations whether they were Kanji or Kana. At times this patient manifested "semantic paralexia" in which confusion took place among Kanji words of related meanings, which is analogous to the compensatory methods of guessing at words in Boder's (1971) dyslexic subgroup I (dysphonetic), semantic substitution errors, which are discussed later. Similar phenomena of semantic paralexia or verbal paraphasia (Geschwind, 1971) have been noted in aphasic patients not only in reading but also in speech.

Differences between left and right parietal dysgraphia and dyslexia (alexia)

Critchley's division of dyslexia into two subtypes: agnosic (spatial) and symbolic (language)

Critchley (1970a) stated that it is possible to distinguish left parietal dysgraphia from right parietal dysgraphia, the latter being characterized by gross defects in spatial arrangements, often with an inordinately broad left margin. Critchley suggested that there may be two types of dyslexia as well—the agnosic type, and the symbolic type. Agnosic dyslexia was said to represent an underlying disorder of spatioconstructional manipulations, whereby geometric and other figures cannot be either assembled or interpreted as letters. Standing in contrast are the more usual cases, in which it is the symbolic nature of the print or writing that cannot be understood—the grapheme-phoneme relationship.

Hécaen's distinction between left and right
parietal alexias and agraphias; analogies
with mathematical difficulties in relation
to left and right-sided lesions

Subdivisions of the dyslexias (alexias) had been noted
by Hécaen (1967) in his discussion of brain mechanisms.
In studies of the parietal lobes he had noted that the
alexias and agraphias of right parietal lesions differ
from those caused by left-sided lesions; the latter bear
on the comprehension or transcription of the graphic code.
The alexias and agraphias due to right parietal lesions are
disturbances in writing and reading which come from perceptual difficulties with the spatial arrangements of letters
and sentences. Spatial dyslexia is characterized not only by
neglect of the left side of the text, and sometimes by neglect
of one or more words (or more likely, of a part of a word),
but also by difficulty in passing from one line to another.
Occipital as well as parietal lesions may be involved. Those
features of right spatial dysgraphias that separate them
from the dysgraphias due to lesions of the left hemisphere
include writing on the right side of the page, inability to
write in a straight line (diagonal or wavy writing), and alterations involving mainly the vertical strokes (m, n, i, v)
and more rarely letters or words. These alterations usually
do not destroy the actual structure of the word, which remains legible, and the grammatical structure of sentences is
never altered. An analogy may be discerned between these
dyslexias-dysgraphias and specific types of difficulty in mathematics resulting from left or right parietal lesions. In
Hécaen's series, mathematical problems caused by figure or
number alexia were significantly more frequent in association with left-sided lesions, but spatial dyscalculia (inability to carry out mathematical operations due to faulty placing of figure or neglect of part of the figures while theoretical principles of operations are preserved) was associated
significantly more frequently with lesions on the right side.
When the problem was anarithmetia (loss of ability to

carry out theoretical operations), lesions were on the right or the left, but somewhat more frequently on the left.

Luria's contribution relating to differences in sequelae of left and right brain lesions

Luria (1973) discussed the differences in pathology between lesions of the left and right hemispheres. Massive lesions of the right parieto-occipital region interfere with processes of spatial gnosis and praxis, a most significant feature of which is unawareness of the left half of the visual field manifested not only when complex drawings are examined during reading, but also in the patient's spontaneous writing and drawing. On the other hand, lesions of the parieto-occipital zones of the left hemisphere at times specifically relate to components of reading from the points of view of higher symbolic processes, complex logical grammatical structures, and also specifically phonetic analysis. Disturbances of phonemic hearing arise only in lesions of the left temporal lobe. At times the principal feature of the clinical picture is that the patient cannot retain even a short series of sounds, syllables, or words in his memory (that is, auditory sequencing difficulty). The patient either confuses their order or simply states that some of the elements of the sequence have been forgotten. Another interesting symptom complex is that caused by lesions of the left parieto-occipital zones which create difficulty in affected patients in the comprehension of syntactic structures. By syntactic or grammatical structures, Luria meant for example prepositional phrases that express relations of space, sequence, or logical concepts, and also the way word order is used in a sentence. A common feature of all these constructions is that all in various ways code logical and not concrete relationships. An example of this pathology would be "summer before spring" rather than the expected "spring before summer." Another characteristic feature of patients with lesions of the left inferior parietal system is that, although they have a good understanding of the meaning of individual words, they cannot grasp the logical meaning of the grammatical construction as a whole. For example, "father's brother" and "brother's father" would mean the same. Particular trouble occurs when word order does not follow the order of meaning, as in "I had breakfast after I had read the newspaper."

Genetic aspects of dyslexia

In those patients with developmental dyslexia of a primary nature, wherein no real evidence of central nervous system damage either pre-, peri-, or postnatally can be obtained, there are often significant family histories. Hereditary factors in primary developmental dyslexia have been suggested since the first cases were described (Rawson, 1968; Critchley, 1970b; Boder, 1971; Klasen, 1972). The more frequent occurrence in boys has been noted for the same period (Critchley, 1970b), ranging in dyslexic groups assessed from one hundred percent to sixty-six percent of the total number. One of the most impressive problems in gathering family data has to do with the reluctance of persons to reveal information, because of "shame" that a member of the family (either the one questioned or his or her offspring) has problems in reading, because accepted ways of thinking in society indicate that the poor reader with no discernible cause is retarded, psychopathologic, poorly motivated, and/or malingering (Rosenthal, 1973a).

Hallgren's Swedish studies; mono- and dizygotic twin studies

The evidence for the genetic aspects of dyslexia is strongest from the Swedish study by Hallgren (1950). In Hallgren's experience, eighty-eight percent of all the probands had one or more relatives with reading problems, often one of the two parents, leading Hallgren to think in terms of an autosomal dominant as the method of inheritance transmission but with perhaps stronger expressivity in males. Furthermore, Hallgren studied twins with dyslexia and strengthening the genetic etiology hypothesis, he noted that of the twelve monozygotic twin pairs, there was one hundred percent concordance for dyslexia. In the thirty-three dizygotic twin pairs, there was thirty-three percent concordance.

Problems with the single-gene model for hereditary dyslexia

Commenting on the concept of the autosomal dominant gene model of Hallgren to explain the familial patterns of dyslexia, Yen and Meredith (1974) indicated that it is not satisfactory for three main reasons: 1) it does not allow for the set ratio of male-to-female dyslexics which is usually about four to one; 2) the model does not account for the occurrence of affected children when neither parent is affected and 3) because of the work of Boder (1971), there is evidence for at least three fundamentally different types of dyslexia (dysphonetic, dyseidetic, and mixed) and therefore the single-gene model does not allow for differences between these three groups. Partial sex-limitation and greater biological vulnerability of the male have been advanced to explain the unbalanced sex ratio and incomplete penetrance in one or both parents is given as an explanation of unexpected affected children. Yen and Meredith feel, however, that a more satisfactory genetic model may develop out of the relation between spatial abilities and the different types of dyslexia. There is evidence, they believe, for a sex-linked recessive gene causing some type of high spatial ability, and it is possible that Boder's dysphonetic Group I contains those persons who have inherited a predisposition for dysphonetic dyslexia which is actuated by the high spatial ability which they have also inherited. In this case "high spatial ability" could be a detriment to successful reading, because it is consistent with letter reversals. If spatially skilled children saw the shapes b/d, p/q as simply rotations of one shape, they might indeed have difficulty in establishing isomorphism between symbols and sounds. They would have difficulty with the law of object constancy, which Money (1962) speaks of as underlying the harmonious development of reading. Yen and Meredith postulated a two-gene model for the one subtype of dyslexia which Boder identified as dysphonetic.

Neurophysiological support for a genetic etiology for developmental dyslexia

In a recent report Conners (1970) has given support to the genetic aspects of dyslexia via neurophysiologic studies. Conners studied a family of poor readers of normal intelligence, and showed that in the father and four children there was an attenuation of the cortical visual evoked response in the left parietal areas. But in the mother, who was the only normal reader in the family, visually evoked responses were normal. Conners suggested that perhaps the neurophysiologic alterations of the information processing capabilities of this area were genetically determined. It would have been interesting to know whether the dyslexics in this family were of a single Boder subgroup, and if so of which one.

Sex-linked differences in cerebral processing

Turner's syndrome

Sex-linked differences in cerebral processing methods of visuospatial tasks have been noted. Thus far the most striking example relates to the report of Money (1966) concerning patients with Turner's syndrome. Patients with this syndrome (gonadal dysgenesis) have only forty-five chromosomes, the missing one being an X of the XX pair. Their karyotype is therefore XO. They cannot reproduce because of rudimentary development of their ovaries. Money noticed that these patients showed visuoconstructional deficits, loss of space form, and impairment of directionality sense, all of which would be expected to be related to subsequent reading and writing difficulties.

In a corroborative study, Bekker and Van Gemund (1968) studied fourteen patients with Turner's syndrome. Although full scale WISC scores were not significantly different from the expected normal curve distribution, the authors did find lower performance than verbal WISC scores in their patients, but only in those older than thirteen. However, nine of the patients with Turner's syndrome, when matched for age and IQ with a control group of girls, showed significantly poorer results on tests such as the Benton Visual Retention Test, the Road Map Test, and the Harris Human Figure Drawings. Bekker and Van Gemund's conclusions were that it was reasonable to suppose that in XO Turner's syndrome there exists a syndrome of spatial-relations-dysgnosia which might be founded upon a neurologically based (genetically as well?) retarded development of body-image which finds expression in weak spatial orientation, poor right-left discrimination, and learning difficulties such as dyscalculia and dyslexia. Specific research in Turner's syndrome with relation to clinical, neurophysiological, and genetic variables is now under way (Meredith, 1975).

Differential language and spatial skills in males and females

McGlone and Kertesz (1973) reported studies on seventy-eight neurological patients with unilateral brain damage in whom they noted right hand preference. Fifty-seven patients had sustained left hemispheric lesions (thirty-five males, twenty-two females) and twenty-one had sustained right hemispheric lesions (thirteen males, eight females). More patients with left than with right hemispheric lesions were seen because the subjects came from an aphasic unit. Lesions included those due to cerebrovascular accidents, neoplastic, degenerative, and traumatic lesions. As expected, speech disturbances were more severe after left than after right-sided lesions, whereas spatial deficits were worse in the right than in the left damaged group. The results suggested basic sex differences in the asymmetrical neural processing of spatial material because, although in both men and women spatial impairment was greater in those with right hemisphere injury than in those with left hemisphere injury, this impairment was greater in males, suggesting that the right hemisphere might be more specialized for spatial processes in men than in women. Thus, new evidence from this study shows that verbal processes may play a significant role in "nonverbal activities" and that females may make more use of this type of verbal mediation. McGlone and Kertesz reviewed data which indicate that females have generally more developed language skills, while they usually perform more poorly than men in a variety of visuospatial tasks. Perhaps these data might suggest differential remedial techniques with relation to the sex of the dyslexic patient and with relation to the subtypes of dyslexia recently described (Boder, 1971).

V

Subgroups of Primary Developmental Dyslexia

Johnson and Myklebust's categories: auditory and visual dyslexics

In recent years, once developmental dyslexia was recognized as a distinct diagnostic category different from mental retardation, psychopathology, poor motivation, and/or malingering, subgroups have been identified, usually those of *visual dyslexia* and *auditory dyslexia*. Johnson and Myklebust (1967), explaining the problems of the auditory dyslexic, described how, although he or she may be able to associate the word *milk* with the liquid in a carton, the patient still can not relate the visual components of the word to their auditory equivalents. They manifest problems with auditory discrimination, analysis and synthesis, and sequencing. The visual dyslexic, on the other hand, usually cannot learn the word as a whole and has problems with visual discrimination, memory, analysis, synthesis, and sequencing, and tends to make reversals in reading, writing, and spelling.

Kinsbourne and Warrington's categories:
a language retardation group
and a Gerstmann group

Kinsbourne and Warrington (1966) and Kinsbourne (1973) studied a group of thirteen slow readers and were able to divide them into subgroups on the basis of at least a twenty point disparity between their verbal and performance IQ scores on the WISC. Group I was a language-retardation group with a lower verbal than performance IQ, who showed other language problems such as disorders in verbalization and receptive language difficulties. The children of this group were often males, had a positive family history for learning difficulty, few or no soft signs on neurological examination, and were rather slow to acquire language. Group II, the Gerstmann group with lower performance than verbal IQ, showed specific problems on tests of finger differentiation and order as well as impaired performance on constructional tasks and mechanical arithmetic, but had neither expressive nor receptive speech or language disorders. This group was composed of children, as often male as female, in whom soft signs did appear on neurological examination, as well as left-right discrimination problems and sequence confusions in letters, causing misreading and misspelling and also poor visual memory. These children misread and misspelled by using letters that sounded right, implying that they were "attacking" the word phonetically.

Bateman's categories: visual learners, auditory
learners, children with deficits in both visual
and auditory skills; therapeutic implications

Bateman (1968), on the basis of characteristic test profiles on the ITPA, identified three subgroups among children with reading disabilities: 1) those who have poor auditory memory but good visual memory, 2) those with poor visual memory but good auditory memory, and 3) those with deficits in both visual and auditory memory whose reading disability is severe and persistent. Bateman suggested that remedially, a sight-word method of reading instruction might be used for Group 1, a phonics approach would be best for Group 2, and a tactile-kinesthetic approach for Group 3.

Boder's subgroups: dysphonetic, dyseidetic, and mixed; Boder clarified interrelations among writing, reading, and spelling errors; created a diagnostic test for dyslexia and its subgroups eliminating the need for diagnosis by exclusion; therapeutic implications; sex ratios and percentages of patients in each subgroup; genetic aspects

The recent work of Boder (1968, 1971) has defined certain subgroups in heterogeneous groups of dyslexic subjects which have theoretical importance but also create insights with relation to therapy. Boder's greatest contribution has been to develop a specific test to diagnose dyslexia and its subgroups, and thus raise it from the confusion of previously being "only a diagnosis by exclusion." In addition, Boder has succeeded in uniting under one diagnostic category the problems not only in reading, but also in spelling and in writing which dyslexic subjects show.

Stressing that the writing-reading-spelling patterns of dyslexic children have diagnostic, prognostic, and therapeutic implications, Boder defined her three groups as follows:

I. *Dysphonetic-dyslexic Group.* Children who reflect problems with sound-symbol integration and difficulties in developing "phonics skills." Lacking phonetic skills (grapheme-phoneme matching), they are unable to sound out, or to blend, the component letters or syllables of a word. They tend to read words better in context than separately, and tend to guess at words from minimal clues; they may select one that is close in meaning but phonetically different from the word they are attempting to read. These are semantic substitution errors, such as "funny" for "laugh," "human" for "person," "answer" for "ask," "quack" for "duck," "airplane" for "train," or "Los Angeles" for "city." Being unable to auditorize, the patient of this group reads by sight and spells correctly to dictation only those words in his sight vocabulary that he can revisualize. Typical spelling errors are inclusion of extraneous and inappropriate letters, and syllable omissions. This child typically has a limited sight vocabulary of whole words that he recognizes and reads fluently. In severe cases the sight vocabulary of an adolescent may not go beyond the fourth or fifth grade levels. Remedial reading techniques, stressing those of "sight-see" approaches, may help. These children tend to persist in the Gestalt approach, preferring to guess at unfamiliar words rather than to employ word analysis and synthesis.

II. *Dyseidetic-dyslexic Group.* Children in this group read laboriously, as though seeing each word for the first time. They have difficulties in learning what the letters look like. Although they can recite the alphabet easily, they may not be able to recognize or write the letters until the fourth or fifth grade. They have little visual memory, and read "by ear" using a groping process of phonetic analysis, and sounding out familiar as well as unfamiliar combinations of letters, rather than by visual-whole-word Gestalts. The child of this group spells poorly but not bizarrely. In contrast to the members of Group I, he and others can readily identify the original word in his spelling list. Examples are "sed" for "said," "lisn" for "listen," "rit" for "right," "bisnis" for "business," and "sos" for "sauce." A striking finding in this group is that nonphonetic words in this child's limited sight vocabulary are often written incorrectly but phonetic words, even when unfamiliar, may be written correctly. Such a child can often spell better than he can read. Remedial techniques stress phonic strengths rather than visual memory weaknesses.

An interesting example of this problem is that of a brilliant but dyslexic (dyseidetic) professor of mathematics who loves to teach algebra but hates to teach geometry because of the many problems in visual memory and spatial configurations he manifests, especially when he draws diagrams on the board.

III. *Mixed Dysphonetic-dyseidetic Dyslexia.* This group comprises a hard core of dyslexic children and often adults who have difficulties both with phonics and with visual memory. They cannot read, spell, or write, either by "ear" or by "eye." The occasional word that a member of this group can recognize on sight or can write is typically at the primer or preprimer level. Characteristically, even with multisensorial approaches such as visual-auditory, and especially tactile-kinesthetic, the response to remedial reading is painfully slow. The Group III child or adult can be differentiated from members of Group I by the much lower grade level of his sight vocabulary and from those of Group II by lack of word analysis skills. His sense of defeat and phobic withdrawal from reading and writing tasks are striking.

In a preliminary study (Boder, 1968), of a total sample of sixty-one dyslexic children, fifty-seven were boys and four were girls. Of the sixty-one patients, sixty-one percent fell into Group I, fifteen percent into Group II, and sixteen percent into Group III; eight percent fell into an "undetermined group." Boder indicated that there were no noticeable sex differences in each of her three groups, and that generally with relation to familial patterns there were no overlaps between the dysphonetic and dyseidetic groups, but that the dysphonetic and mixed groups showed overlap, that is, both subgroups were found in the same family (Boder, 1975).

VI

Secondary Psychological Effects of Primary Developmental Dyslexia

Feelings of frustration, poor self-concept, and aggressive antisocial behavior

Almost every author who has written about developmental dyslexia has commented on the profound secondary emotional disturbances in these subjects who cannot read without discernible cause. An unfortunate reaction which dyslexics show at times is aggression. Critchley (1970b) quoted the work of Edmond Critchley, who in 1968 studied the possible relations between dyslexia and juvenile delinquency. He investigated the incidence of reading disability in a Remand Home and Classifying Centre for the twelve Inner London Boroughs. In a group of 106 delinquent boys studied prospectively and 371 studied retrospectively, ranging in age from 12 to 17 years, he found that 60 percent were delayed in reading by two years or more, and 50 percent by more than three years. Probably a good many had reading problems because of socio-motivational factors. However, some almost certainly had primary developmental dyslexia. Nonetheless, there seemed to be a high correlation between acted-out antisocial aggression and problems in reading.

Orton (1937), in his classic work on reading, writing, and speech problems in children, described emotional and personality disturbances secondary to the social trauma of reading incompetence. These secondary effects include feelings of frustration, inferiority, instability, neuroticism, and rebellious acting out.

*Seldom do emotional problems cause learning
failures; rather they are effects*

Rawson (1968) observed that few of her patients were free of emotional problems such as low self-esteem and personal tension; she also noted that the emotional problems seldom appeared to cause learning failures but were effects of these failures. She stressed that problems of low self-esteem in a group of boys were more prevalent and persistent among those who were given help *after* they had experienced failure than among those who were helped *before* failure.

Self-esteem lower in a group of dyslexics whose
families lacked understanding of the term

Rosenthal (1973b) studied twenty dyslexic boys and found that they had significantly less self-esteem, as shown by Coopersmith Self-Esteem Inventories (Coopersmith, 1967), than control groups of normals and asthmatics. In addition Rosenthal divided his dyslexic group into two subgroups of ten boys each:

1. Dyslexia No Mystery (DNM): The family understood the problem because the diagnosis had been made before in another family member or in a close friend.
2. Dyslexia Mystery (DM): the family had no experience with or understanding of the term, the problem, and its consequences.

There were significantly lower self-esteem levels in the DM subgroup than in the DNM subgroup, suggesting that lack of information leads to anxiety and guilt in the family

and to low self-esteem in the patient. In parent inter-
views later on, it was noted that information about dyslexia
changed family attitudes. For example, it led to more
sympathy and understanding of these troubled children.

VII

Neurophysiological Studies—Concepts of Cerebral Hemispheric Specialization: Relations to Developmental Dyslexia

Previous EEG studies not specifically diagnostic

Until recently, neurophysiological studies attempting to establish correlations between specific *reading disabilities* and EEG tracings have not been particularly helpful (Klasen, 1973), even though the incidence of abnormal EEGs is higher in children with *minimal brain dysfunction* than in normal controls (Boder, 1971). Critchley (1970b), reviewing EEG studies in dyslexia, noted that mild dysrhythmias suggestive of cortical immaturity are often found, which may be most evident in the parieto-occipital areas bilaterally. Among the problems in the interpretation of EEG data which Critchley mentioned are the coexisting positive neurological findings which are more conspicuous in younger dyslexics, and the confused diagnostic standards for dyslexia in older groups, wherein psychiatric overlays are quite prominent.

Concept of delayed maturation in dyslexia

The concepts of *maturation* from cognitive, neurophysiological and emotional points of view in dyslexia must be taken into consideration even though the parameters of maturation are extremely difficult to assess. Yet some "dyslexics" at age six to eight suddenly do not belong any more in that diagnostic category at ages eight to ten. Delayed maturation or neurodevelopmental lags or "late-bloomers" do exist clinically even though they are hard to define psychoeducationally or neuroanatomically.

Subclinical reading epilepsy?

One EEG study (not corroborated by two other attempts at replication) is noteworthy if speculative. Critchley cited the studies of Baro and Oettinger, who found that EEG abnormalities were actually precipitated by the *attempts* to read texts just beyond the subject's comprehension, in that the EEG showed a dysrhythmia which became progressively worse with increasingly difficult words and phrases, to the point that the EEG pattern took on epileptic qualities, suggesting subclinical reading epilepsy.

Auditory evoked cortical potentials in children with MBD: visual evoked cortical potentials in a family of dyslexics; relations between neurophysiological measures of delayed maturation and clinically observed immature behavior

Satterfield et al (1973), working with thirty-one children with minimal brain dysfunction (MBD, but the group was not diagnostically defined as having developmental dyslexia) and twenty-one normal controls, matched for age and sex, found that auditory evoked cortical potentials in the MBD group had significantly lower amplitudes and longer latencies than those in the control group. As mentioned above, Conners (1970) found markedly diminished left-sided visual cortical evoked potentials in a family of poor readers. Satterfield stressed that the most common clinical EEG abnormality found in MBD children is an excessive amount of slow wave activity and this, like the increased latency of the evoked response, is consistent with delayed maturation of the central nervous system, which in turn is consistent with the clinically observed immature behavior of these MBD children, all suggesting an underlying neurophysiological basis for the disorders seen in these children.

In dyslexic children EEG spectral analysis
showed greater mean coherences for all
activity within the same hemisphere but in normals
the coherences tended to be higher between
symmetrical regions across the midline

Recognizing that there are differences between the EEGs of dyslexics and normals, but that refinements of technique were required, Sklar (1971) examined twelve dyslexics (ten boys, two girls, aged nine to eighteen years) in whom all of Boder's three subgroups were represented, but most were of Subgroup I (dysphonetic). The EEGs were evaluated not by direct visual inspection, but by a computer search for disparities, following which a computer classification of normal and dyslexic children was rendered, using spectral estimates of their EEGs. Sklar found that the two groups could be differentiated especially during the rest, eyes-closed phase. The most prominent spectral differences appeared in the parieto-occipital region; the dyslexic children on the average had more energy in the 3-7 Hz and 16-32 Hz bands—the normals, in the 9-14 Hz band (Hz refers to a unit of frequency in the EEG equal to one cycle per second). However, during the actual reading task the autospectral disparity between the two sample populations was reversed at 16-32 Hz, in that here, normals had greater energy. The mean coherences for all activity within the same hemisphere were higher for dyslexics, whereas the coherences tended to be higher for normals between symmetrical regions across the midline. However, if the EEG, or more specifically, the coherences between hemispheres, is taken as an index of the transfer of information in the central nervous system, then the greatest differences between normals and dyslexics might have been expected to occur during the reading task, rather than during the state of rest, eyes-closed.

EEG coherence findings in adult dyslexics
similar to those of children; Hanley feels that
he can distinguish dyslexics from normals by
visual inspection of the standard EEG

Hanley (1975), working with adult dyslexics (not subgrouped according to the Boder classification) noted that in general, the findings with respect to shared activity as calculated from the coherence function were similar to those in children, in that those without dyslexia showed greater shared activity between symmetrical placements across the hemispheres. Hanley took this to be valuable evidence of the robustness of the coherence findings in the face of known maturational processes in the EEG in the progression from childhood to adulthood. In addition, Hanley believed he could visually assess the standard EEG without computer aid and diagnose dyslexia. He believed that dyslexics generate more theta activity from the parieto-occipital areas bilaterally than do nondyslexics, and that the dyslexics show at the same time broad-band alpha, which is poorly defined and spread out over the 8-14 Hz band.

Recent neurophysiological research

The subgrouping of dyslexia has given this complicated area definition, suggestions for remediation and in a sense respectability. In addition, a most promising approach has to do with neurophysiological advances with relation to specialized hemispheric functioning in different cognitive and perceptual tasks.

Obtaining reflections of the relations between
ongoing neurophysiological and cognitive states

Callaway (1973) has shown that there are positive correlations between average evoked potentials and more conventional measures of intelligence but perhaps more importantly these positive correlations show that one can obtain a reflection of the relation between ongoing neurophysiological and cognitive states. Callaway found that brighter subjects show shorter latencies, asymmetry in that the right evoked response is greater than the left, lower evoked potential variability, and plasticity of the evoked response. The plasticity will correlate with intelligence only when intelligent subjects would be expected to be more plastic in that they would be *expected* to show more change than the less bright, from task to task in their cognitive response. The relation between evoked potentials and intelligence probably reflects the differences in subjects' ongoing cognitive processes rather than hard-wired differences in neurophysiological organization.

Preferred cognitive modes as determined by
evoked potential and EEG studies; subjects not
at rest but performing verbal and spatial tasks;
interference hypothesis with relation to inefficient
cognitive styles; support for Orton's theory of lack
of cerebral lateral specialization as the cause for
dyslexia? Are the dysphonetics and dyseidetics
extreme versions neurophysiologically of those
markedly dysfunctioned in auditory (verbal-left)
and visual (spatial-right) cognitive styles?

Galin and Ellis (1975) felt that asymmetries in evoked potential amplitude might be in part dependent on asymmetries in the alpha amplitude of the background EEG, which the authors believed to be a function of the particular and preferred cognitive mode the subject is using. Galin and Ellis recorded flash evoked potentials and background EEG in six right-handed adults from left and right temporal and parietal areas not while the subjects were "at rest," but rather while they performed specific verbal (writing from memory) and spatial (modified Kohs Block Design) tasks. Previous studies had shown that in spatial tasks (right hemisphere) the alpha ratio (right/left) was lower than in verbal tasks (left hemisphere); the hemisphere engaged by the task develops proportionately less alpha power. In this study the authors found that the overall power and peak amplitude characteristics of the evoked potential asymmetry reflected lateralization of cognitive processes but not as consistently as the concomitant asymmetry in EEG alpha power. If both EEG and evoked potential asymmetry measures reflect the hemispheric specialization of verbal-left and spatial-right cognitive tasks, it would be most interesting to test the Boder subgroup dyslexics (dysphonetic and dyseidetic) via these measures to see whether a relation could be found between clinical expressions of a cognitive problem and neurophysiological substrate differences.

Galin and Ornstein (1973) indicated that in many ordinary activities, normal people simply alternate between cognitive modes rather than integrate them. Although it is possible to process complex spatial relationships in words, it would seem more efficient to use visual-kinesthetic images. Galin and Ornstein gave the example of what most do when asked to describe a spiral staircase—they begin to use words but quickly fall back on gesturing with a finger because here gesture is more efficient. An "interference hypothesis" has arisen to describe a situation in which an inefficient and inappropriate cognitive style is being used to process a certain task while at the same time preventing the more efficient mode from working. This interference between the right and left cognitive modes has generated new support for Orton's (1925) theory that lack of cerebral lateral specialization plays a major role in the etiology of dyslexia. The implication for education is that an individual's preferred cognitive style, which may possibly now be assessed by EEG and evoked cortical potential measures, may facilitate his learning of one type of subject matter, such as spatial-relational, while hampering the learning of another type, such as verbal-analytic. A student's difficulty with reading when only a phonics (left?) or wholeword-Gestalt (right?) teaching approach is used may arise from his inability to change to the cognitive mode required of him. Perhaps the subgroups of dyslexics (Boder's dysphonetic, dyseidetic) are extreme versions, neurophysiologically and genetically based, of these inabilities to alternate or to integrate cognitive styles.

Different cognitive modes for different
socioeconomic groups? A reason for
intergroup misunderstanding?

It appears that subcultures in the United States are characterized by predominant cognitive modes which might be related to Bernstein's (1964) restricted and elaborated codes of language and cognitive styles for different socioeconomic groups. The middle class tends to use verbal-analytic cognitive modes, while the urban poor are more likely to use spatial-holistic modes. This may be a cause of misunderstanding between the groups and a reason that the urban poor have troubles in school systems oriented towards the middle class.

Coupling measures between cortical areas assess
central nervous system information processing;
appositional right hemisphere processing increases
couplings between the occiput and the right
hemisphere; propositional left hemisphere processing
increases coupling to the left hemisphere

Callaway and Harris (1974) have described a new way to assess how the central nervous system processes data by measuring coupling between cortical areas. When two areas of the brain are in active functional communication, then some relationship should exist between the EEGs from these two areas. The two EEGs can at any instant be classified on the basis of polarity and direction of change of potential (that is, slope), and the results of such a classification can be used to measure coupling. Functional communications between visual area and each of the left and right hemispheres were manipulated by assigning verbal (left hemisphere) and spatial (right hemisphere) tasks to nine right-handed subjects. Their results indicated that appositional (right hemisphere) processing of visual data (examining a picture) tends to increase coupling between the occiput and the right hemisphere; and propositional (read silently-left hemisphere) processing tends to increase coupling to the left. Changes in EEG coupling that accompany changes in cognitive processing support the idea that the EEG is actually related to electrical events involved in information processing of the central nervous system, and this approach, the authors felt, is suitable as an alternative to more conventional time series measures such as cross-spectra and coherences for studying relations between the EEG and brain information processing.

Cortical coupling techniques showed that left-right ratio for clicks was greater than the left-right ratio for flashes for frontal-parietal lead pairs; preliminary study with dyslexics: reversal of results in normals

Bali et al. (1975) cited the work of Davis and Wada, who measured coherences between average evoked potentials recorded from temporal and parietal leads and found that clicks induced more coherence in the speech dominant hemisphere than on the other side, and that flashes produced more coherence in the other, non-speech dominant hemisphere. Bali et al. replicated the Davis and Wada data by using the same stimulus paradigm but a method of EEG analysis by cortical coupling. In right-handed subjects, the left-right ratio for clicks was found to be greater than the left-right ratio for flashes for frontal-parietal lead pairs. In addition there was one interesting sex difference—females tended to have greater left-right coupling ratios than males. This was true for flashes and clicks with the simple measure but only for clicks with the partialled measure.

Potential application of this relatively simple method of EEG cortical coupling analysis is in the confusing area of dyslexia, the clinical subgroups of which imply etiologies pertaining to functional differences or at least different cognitive modes between the left and right hemispheres. In a preliminary study, Bali et al. (1975), working with eleven older dyslexics (not divided into clinical subgroups) found a reversal of their results obtained with normals. Nine of the eleven dyslexics showed left-right ratios of coupling higher for flash than for clicks.

VIII

Three Out-of-the-Mainstream Approaches to Writing-Reading Difficulties: Theories Relating to Causes and Remediation

Three models which purport to explain reading, writing and dysfunctions thereof and which are essentially not in the conventional mainstream of relevant teaching and research should be mentioned if only because of the marked controversies they have engendered.

The method of Doman and Delacato: for a wide spectrum of disabilities; concept of neurological organization; patterning techniques; nonreplication of results by others

Doman and Delacato (associated with the Institute for the Achievement of Human Potential at Philadelphia) have presented a "patterning" theory and technique for the treatment of many types of brain damage, which is based on the principle that ontogeny recapitulates phylogeny. It follows, according to the thinking of Doman and Delacato, that failure to pass properly through a certain sequence of developmental stages in mobility, language, and competence in the manual, visual, auditory, and tactile areas reflects poor "neurological organization" and may indicate brain damage (Freeman, 1967). Doman and Delacato indicated that they can reach the brain itself by pouring stimuli into the afferent-sensory system in intensities and frequencies gauged to reap responses in corresponding motor systems. In addition to "patterning" procedures, which in severely brain-damaged patients require manipulation via passive movements by several persons, their techniques may include rebreathing of expired air, restrictions on the intake of fluids, salt, and sugar, the early learning of reading (age two years if possible), and techniques aimed at establishing uniform cortical hemispheric dominance which include restrictions on hand use, eye use, or exposure to music because music and tonal stimulation are presumed to evoke responses in the nondominant cerebral hemisphere. In addition there are certain required positions with relation to sleep and rest, and there are visual and gait training procedures. A very controversial element of Doman and Delacato's contention is that progress in one functional area will result in improvements in other potential abilities. For example, they contend that gains in mobility patterns will, without specific remediation in speech areas, lead to improvement in expressive language. They do not, however, consider these gains in relation to possibilities of the Hawthorne, or novelty, effect. Other requirements of the Doman-Delacato program include certain lateralizing maneuvers such as training the child to use an appropriate sleep position, that is, the prone position with the face turned toward the nondominant hand with the arms and legs in the "fencing position" towards the non-dominant side of the body. In color-filtration activities, a red translucent plastic lens is placed over the nondominant eye. During writing activities, a red pencil is used. The red lens over the nondominant eye filters out the image so that only the dominant eye can detect what is being written. During reading, green cellophane is placed over the book, causing the image to be filtered out by the red lens, so that only the dominant eye is able to detect the printed material (Robbins, 1966).

Because of the claim that the "Doman-Delacato Patterning Method" achieved success in such diverse problems as frank brain injury, improper environmental opportunities, inadequate mobility, poor handwriting, hyperactivity, delayed speech, articulation disorders, stuttering, aphasia, spelling difficulties, reading problems, and low scores on college entrance examination, Robbins (1967) made an empirical test of the central concept and the treatment efficacy of the Doman-Delacato rationale. A group of retarded readers was compared with appropriate control groups. There was no statistically significant difference in mean reading scores among good, fair, and poor creepers. In addition, reading was not related to laterality, and reading improvement was not related to the experimental Doman-Delacato Program, which included among its requirements cross-pattern creeping, cross-pattern walking, and elimination of all musical activities.

*The optometric visual treatment approach
to children with reading problems;
optometrists and ophthalmologists
often disagree*

Another area of great controversy resulting in confusion and antipathy among proponents of several disciplines has to do with validity studies relating to the optometric visual treatment approaches to children with reading problems. Usually, but not always, the optometrists and the ophthalmologists are opposed in their thinking on this issue. Notwithstanding the difficulties encountered in attempts to define such terms as reading problem, reading incompetence, reading retardation, dyslexia, motor-perceptual dysfunction, visual-perceptual lag, and so forth, some relatively clear positions have been juxtaposed.

Outlining the component processes of reading as visual (retino-occipital), perceptual (parieto-occipital), and conceptual (frontal lobes), Goldberg (1968) believed that there is little relation between visual ability per se and the reading problem based on dysfunctions of symbol interpretation. In discussing his series from the Wilmer Institute in Baltimore, Goldberg compared the visual, fusional, and muscle findings and accommodative convergence ratios determined in dyslexic patients with those of a group of normal readers and saw no statistically significant differences. Nicholls (1960) was also of the opinion that only infrequently is dyslexia primarily an ocular problem, but he did indicate that a detailed ocular motility study, both motor and sensory, is required in a differential diagnosis. Orthoptic training occasionally may be indicated when there are fusional difficulties. Specific treatment should be given for firm diagnoses of myopia, hyperopia, esophoria, and heterotropia. Interestingly, and in contradistinction to the approach of Doman and Delacato in further strengthening the dominant eye by various techniques, Nicholls reinforced the ophthalmological principle of occlusion of the dominant eye for correction of amblyopia or "lazy eye" by forcing the weaker eye to work.

Benton's finding of many dyslexics with binocular control abnormalities; overlapping diagnostic categories and a multiplicity of treatment approaches cause great difficulty in evaluating results

Benton (1968) studied a group of 1,500 children in whom he made the diagnosis of dyslexia because they manifested selective retardation of reading skills, resulting in an observable gap between a child's progress in reading and his progress in other areas of learning. In

77 percent of this group of dyslexics a subtype of dyslexia was found, characterized by binocular control abnormalities. Among the remaining 33 percent, according to Benton's classification, 10 percent of the total group had primary dyslexia (developmental dyslexia, congenital word blindness); 8 percent had dyslexia associated with organic neurologic behavior syndrome (concomitant hyperactivity); 5 percent had dyslexia secondary to functional or environmental factors (cultural deprivation, lack of motivation, overcrowded schools, hearing and speech defects, emotional problems, conventional ophthalmologic problems). The diagnosis of binocular control abnormalities was made by establishing that these children had crossed dominance (right-handed/left-eyed, or left-handed/right-eyed), or alternating intermittent macular suppression as measured by stereoscopic examination using retinal rival targets. Benton, as support for his thesis, had noted that dyslexia was rare in monocular children. Fifteen of these children who had lost the sight of one eye since infancy were all good readers. In addition, Benton noted that some dyslexic children appear to read faster when one eye is occluded. In another series, Benton noted that after the correction of the strabismus in 97 children with esotropia, the incidence of dyslexia rose from 8 percent to 19 percent.

Management for the children with binocular control abnormalities included the attempt to change hand ambidexterity to fully one-sided functioning, and the encouragement of kicking with the foot on the side of the dominant hand. Eye training was directed to the eye on the side of the dominant hand. Between the ages of five and ten years, constant occlusion of the eye which should be nondominant was instituted. When tests suggested that control was changing, the wearing time of the patch was progressively reduced. Because children from ages ten to sixteen years usually will not consent to wear a patch, atropine was instilled daily into the eye that should be nondominant.

Using no controls, Benton treated 700 dyslexic children with binocular control abnormalities for periods ranging from 9 to 24 months by the management techniques enumerated above. Excellent improvement was reported in 49 percent (336 children) with respect to attaining grade level in reading, reading for pleasure, disappearance of behavior problems, and gain in bodily coordination skills; 50 percent of the 336 children changed their dominance pattern to homolaterality. Those children who did not improve in reading skills showed no change in dominance patterns. In addition to fostering homolateral eye and hand dominance, Benton used *adjunctive programs;* this addition makes it difficult to establish significant causal relationships. Included in the adjunctive programs were remedial reading, neuromuscular coordination exercises, skill games, and sleep positioning, drug treatment, and the elimination of music.

Seiderman's (1972) report of success in improving reading scores via perceptual-motor and optometric approaches is also difficult to assess because of the multiplicity of therapeutic modalities involved. In addition to pursuit and saccadic training, stereoscopic pointing techniques, cheiroscopic tracings (methods of training binocular vision), and work with the electronic localizer to improve visual motor coordination, Seiderman employed inputs via remedial reading techniques, gross-motor training, form perception techniques, and exercises in seriation, classification, sorting, cause and effect reasoning, and sequential thinking. No appropriate controls were used, nor were the effects of normal development taken into account.

Swanson's use of prisms and lenses to enhance
binocular vision in contradistinction to Benton's
thesis stressing advantages of monocular vision

In reviewing one hundred cases of learning disorders, seventy-three percent of which included dyslexia, Swanson

(1972) cited the beneficial effects of optometric vision therapy in ninety-three percent. Noting problems of hyperopia, astigmatism, inadequate focus flexibility, low focus amplitudes, improper accommodative convergence ratios, and excessive esophoria, Swanson made extensive use of lenses and prisms so that the eyes would focus closer as well as farther away; in addition, he moved the projected image up or down, in or out. In contradistinction to Benton's thesis, the lenses and prisms were employed to force the person to use both eyes; they also trained hand-eye coordination. Swanson used Polaroid and anaglyph (eyeglasses whose two lenses are of different colors, used to view composite pictures printed in the same two colors, producing a three-dimensional effect) lenses to enhance binocular vision and stereopsis because "it is an accepted fact that anything interfering with the coordination of the two eyes shortens the attention span and interferes with the memory process. It is considered by some to be the nucleus of the learning processes." In Swanson's work many other treatment modalities—educational, psychological, and medical—were concurrently in effect, so that his results are difficult to assess.

Saccadic movements: increases in fixations and
regressions; probably the results rather than causes
of poor reading; oculonystagmographic (measurements
of involuntary movements of the eyeball) studies;
Goldberg's thoughts about reconstructed perceptual
clues closely akin to Werner's principle of
microgenesis; studies of saccadic eye movements
with nonreading material—results not clear because
of limitations of experimental design

Griffin et al (1974) reviewed the work of Javal, who in 1878 noted that the eyes of a school child swept along a line of print, not in a steady sweep, but in a series of little jumps (saccadic movements), with intervening fixation pauses. Subsequent studies of saccadic eye movments during reading consistently indicated that the eyes of poor readers made more fixations of longer duration and more regressions than did the eyes of good readers at elementary, secondary, and college levels. Conventional thinking in this area has been that the increased number and increased variability of the saccades were the results rather than the causes of poor reading. Goldberg (1968) is a proponent of the concept that faulty eye movements and inefficient fixations are the results of poor comprehension of written language. Working with the oculonystagmograph, Goldberg charted eye movements by measuring changes in retino-corneal electrical potentials. Deviations from established norms occurred in oculonystagmograms when good readers attempted unfamiliar words and when brain-damaged children groped for the understanding of a word. Confirming the central rather than the peripheral cause for the aberrant rhythms in the oculonystagmograms, when a third grade reader was helped with unfamiliar and difficult sixth-grade words, a normal tracing of eye movements was achieved. When help with new words was withheld, the child reverted to hesitant, paced, repetitive fixations. Goldberg indicated that visual, then perceptual clues come from individual letters, symbols, and words, which are rapidly reconstructed to create a general pattern. The better the reader, the fewer clues are needed. This concept seems closely akin to the principle of microgenesis, proposed by Werner (Baldwin, 1967), which states that within the fraction of a second that is required to perceive an object, that perception develops from an early undifferentiated perception through a sequence of developmental stages to a differentiated, articulated, and organized one. Werner felt that the perceptions of the young child or the schizophrenic patient (perhaps those of the dyslexic as well) reflect the halting of the normal developmental process. In experiments in microgenesis, showing stimulus words for 1/50 second, Werner pointed out that in some subjects the development of recognition of a word went through a stage wherein the word's general sphere of meaning was apprehended before the word itself was recognizable. The Gestalt came, Werner believed, because the subject, in achieving the final correct perception, engaged in an active, organismic involvement.

In an attempt to show that saccades might be a cause rather than an effect of poor reading, Griffin et al (1974) compared a group of adequate readers with a group of inadequate readers by using nonreading as well as reading material and tasks. Their assumption was that the nonlanguage materials, which included picture, dot, and word cards, did not involve comprehension. This assumption was perhaps unwarranted. At least *perception was* involved. The authors concluded that inadequate readers seemed to have less efficient saccadic eye movements regardless of the type of material used. The inadequate readers, however, comprised a heterogeneous group within which two subgroups emerged, one at each end of the performance spectrum. The first group sequenced saccadic eye movements too rapidly, slipping and omitting material; the second group sequenced saccades too slowly, resulting in overfixations. The authors granted that the heterogeneity of the inadequate reader group might account for difficulties with relation to clearcut statistical results. Other problems with the experimental design pertain to the case histories of the subjects; these did not indicate, for example, whether or not the behavioral syndrome of distractibility, hyperactivity, and decreased attention span coexisted in the group of inadequate readers. This behavioral triad, which can coexist with dyslexia in some patients with learning disabilities, can manifest overactive eye movements as part of the general impulsive motor overflow which these patients display.

Dyslexia caused by cerebellar-vestibular
dysfunction rather than by cortical
dysfunction? Subclinical nystagmus occurs,
causing disordered ocular fixation, disordered
sequential scanning of letters and words,
resulting in letter and word scrambling, that
is, dysmetric dyslexia and dyspraxia

An interesting and innovative approach to dyslexia has recently been reported by Frank and Levinson (1973), who found evidence of a cerebellar-vestibular dysfunction in 97 percent of 115 consecutive dyslexic children referred for psychiatric evaluation because of poor or refractory response to reading instruction. This brain dysfunction was manifested by positive Romberg signs, difficulty in tandem walking, articulatory speech disorders, dysdiado-chokinesis, hypotonia, and dysmetric or past-pointing disturbances during tests of finger-to-nose, heel-to-toe, writing, drawing, ocular fixation, and scanning. Good-enough figure drawings and Bender Gestalt designs revealed disturbed spatial orientation in all of the children. This, and tilting of these drawings from horizontal and vertical axes, as well as steering difficulties during angle formations, suggested impairment of the inner spatial steering and equilibrium mechanism of the vestibular apparatus and cerebellar-vestibular circuits. Twenty-six of 30 randomly selected patients among the 112 with dyslexia manifested electronystagmographic abnormalities and spontaneous and positional nystagmus, dysmetric ocular pursuit, and asymmetric vestibular functioning, while ear, nose, throat, and audiographic findings were normal. The authors planned to test the hypothesis that 1) the cerebellar-vestibular circuits provide a harmonious, well-integrated, and stable motor background for visual perception; 2) this motor "background" or "Gestalt" is the subliminal, automatic, integrated motor activity of the eye muscles, head, and neck, permitting ocular fixation and sequential scanning of letters and words; 3) where there are cerebellar dysfunction and subclinical nystagmus, ocular fixation and sequential scanning of letters and words are disordered and letter and word scrambling results; 4) this scrambling and resulting dysmetric visual perception lead to deficient comprehension or dyslexia; and 5) primary cerebellar-vestibular dysfunction in children, with resultant dysmetric visual perception and accompanying anxiety, may cause maturational lag. The authors suggested the use of cerebellar-vestibular harmonizing agents such as cyclizine, alone or with reticular activating and alerting agents such as methylphenidate, for prevention of dysmetric dyslexia in preschool children with cerebellar-vestibular dysfunction, and for its treatment in school children with that disorder. They asserted that subclinical nystagmus had been convincingly demonstrated electronystagmographically in dysmetric dyslexia, and stated that 2 percent of the first-grade population of Staten Island had dysmetric dyslexia. They added that they had recently proved the dysmetric dyslexic hypothesis by a new, rapid (2-5 minutes per child), 98 percent accurate, and specific dysmetric dyslexic mass screening procedure and instrument capable of detecting cerebellar-vestibular dysfunction and dysmetric dyslexia in prekindergarten (four to five year old) and beginning school children without Barany caloric stimulation.

Since previous experience indicates many subfunctions in the writing-reading-spelling process, and there is good clinical and experimental evidence for subtypes of dyslexia, it is at least at this time difficult to accept such statistically overwhelming data implying one cause for such a complicated problem. Future well-designed experiments coordinating the efforts of the neuropsychologist, clinician, and electrophysiologist will probably clarify the relative position of these findings in the total spectrum of organic and psychological components that make up the life of one who, for no discernible cause, cannot write-read-spell in our society.

Bibliography

Adams, R., Kocsis, J., and Estes, R. "Soft neurological signs in learning disabled children and controls." *American Journal of Diseases of Children* (1974), 128: 614–618.

Ainsworth, M. "The effects of maternal deprivation." In *Deprivation of Maternal Care.* New York: Schocken Books, 1966.

Arnolt, V. "A Piagetian interpretation of reading in early childhood." Paper presented at 5th Invitational Interdisciplinary Seminar on Piagetian Theory and Its Implications for the Helping Professions. University of Southern California, Los Angeles, 1975.

Asch, S. "On the use of metaphor in the description of persons." In *On Expressive Language,* edited by H. Werner. Worcester, Mass.: Clark University Press, 1955.

Ayres, J. *Sensory Integration and Learning Disorders.* Los Angeles: Western Psychological Services, 1972.

Bakwin, H. "Learning problems and school phobia." *Pediatric Clinics of North America* (1965), 12: 995–1014.

Baldwin, A. *Theories of Child Development.* New York: John Wiley & Sons, 1967.

Bali, L., Callaway, E., and Naghdi, S. "Hemispheric asymmetry in cortical coupling for visual and auditory nonverbal stimuli." Langley Porter Neuropsychiatric Institute, University of California Medical Center, San Francisco, 1975. Unpublished data.

Bannatyne, A. *Reading: An Auditory-Vocal Process.* San Rafael, Calif.: Academic Therapy Publications, 1973.

Barlow, C. " 'Soft signs' in children with learning disorders." *American Journal of Diseases of Children* (1974), 128: 605–606.

Bateman, B. *Interpretation of the 1961 Illinois Test of Psycholinguistic Abilities.* Seattle: Special Child Publications, 1960.

Bekker, F., and Van Gemund, J. "Mental retardations and cognitive defects in Turner's syndrome." *Maandschrift voor Kindergeneeskunde* (1968), 36: 148–156.

Benton, C. "Management of dyslexias associated with binocular control abnormalities." In *Dyslexia,* edited by A. Keeney and V. Keeney. St. Louis: The C. V. Mosby Co., 1968

Bernstein, B. "Elaborated and restricted codes: Their social origins and some consequences." In *The Ethnography of Communication,* edited by J. Gumperz and D. Hymes. American Anthropologist Special Publication, Vol. 66, No. 6, Part 2. Menasha, Wisc.: American Anthropologist, 1964.

Birch, H., and Belmont, L. "Auditory-visual integration in normal and retarded readers." *American Journal of Orthopsychiatry* (1964), 34: 852–861.

Blanchard, P. "Psychoanalytic contributions to the problems of reading disabilities." In *The Psychoanalytic Study of the Child,* Vol. 2. New York: International Universities Press, 1946.

Boder, E. "Developmental dyslexia—a diagnostic screening procedure based on 3 characteristic patterns of reading and spelling. A preliminary report." *Claremont Reading Conference 32nd Yearbook.* Claremont, Calif.: Claremont University Center, 1968.

————. "Developmental dyslexia—prevailing diagnostic

concepts and a new diagnostic approach through patterns of reading and spelling." In *Progress in Learning Disabilities*, Vol. 2, edited by H. Myklebust. New York: Grune & Stratton, 1971.

————. Personal communication, 1975.

Bormuth, J. "An operational definition of comprehension instruction." In *Psycholinguistics and the Teaching of Reading*, edited by S. Goodman and J. Fleming. Newark, Del.: International Reading Association, 1969.

Bowlby, J. *Maternal Care and Mental Health*. New York: Schocken Books, 1966.

Braine, M. "The ontogeny of English phrase structure: the first phase." *Language* (1963), 39: 1–13.

Brislawn, F. "Space representation and language development." In *Piagetian Theory and the Helping Professions*, edited by G. Lubin, J. Magary, and M. Poulson. Los Angeles: University of Southern California, 1975.

Brosin, H. "Commentary upon Pollack, I. Language as behavior." In *Brain Mechanisms Underlying Speech and Language*, edited by C. Millikan and F. Darley. New York: Grune & Stratton, 1967.

Calfee, R., and Venezky, R. "Component skills in beginning reading." In *Psycholinguistics and the Teaching of Reading*, edited by K. Goodman and J. Fleming. Newark, Del.: International Reading Association, 1969.

Callaway, E. "Correlations between averaged evoked potentials and measures of intelligence." *Archives of General Psychiatry* (1973), 29: 553–558.

————, and Harris, P. "Coupling between cortical potentials from different areas." *Science* (1974), 183: 873–875.

Chase, R. "Evolutionary aspects of language development and function." In *The Genesis of Language*, edited by F. Smith and G. Miller. Cambridge, Mass.: The MIT Press, 1966.

Chomsky, N. *Aspects of the Theory of Syntax*. Cambridge, Mass.: The MIT Press, 1965.

————. "Linguistic contributions to the study of the mind—history." *Beckman Lecture Series*, Part I. Berkeley, Calif.: Academic Publishing Co., 1967.

Cleator, P. *Lost Languages*. New York: The John Day Co., 1961.

Clements, S. *Minimal Brain Dysfunctions in Children*. National Institute of Neurological Diseases and Blindness Monograph No. 3., Washington, D.C.: U.S. Department of Health, Education, and Welfare; U.S. Government Printing Office, 1966.

Condon, W., and Ogston, W. "A segmentation of behavior." *Journal of Psychiatric Research* (1967), 5: 221–235.

Conners, K. "Cortical visual-evoked response in children with learning disorders." *Psychophysiology* (1970), 7: 418–428.

Coopersmith, S. *The Antecedents of Self Esteem*. San Francisco: W. H. Freeman & Co., 1967.

Cravioto, J., and Delicardie, E. "Mental performance in school age children: Findings after recovery from early severe malnutrition." *American Journal of Diseases of Children* (1970), 120: 404–410.

Crawford, S. Personal communication, 1972.

Critchley, M. "Isolation of the specific dyslexic." In *Dyslexia*, edited by A. Keeney and V. Keeney. St. Louis: The C. V. Mosby Co., 1968.

————. *Aphasiology*. London: Edward Arnold Publishers, Ltd., 1970a.

————. *The Dyslexic Child*. Springfield, Ill.: Charles C Thomas, 1970b.

d'Alviella, G. *The Migration of Symbols*. New York: University Books, 1894 (reproduced 1956).

Dance, F. "Toward a theory of human communication." In *Human Communication Theory*, edited by F. Dance. New York: Holt, Rinehart and Winston, 1967.

Davison, L. Introduction. In *Clinical Neuropsychology;*

Current Status and Applications, edited by R. Reitan and L. Davison. Washington, D.C.: V. H. Winton & Sons, 1974.

De Hirsch, K., Jansky, J., and Langford, W. *Predicting Reading Failure.* New York: Harper & Row, 1966.

Eisenberg, L. "Reading retardation: Psychiatric and sociologic aspects." *Pediatrics* (1966), 37: 352–365.

Ekman, P., and Friesen, W. "Hand movements." *Journal of Communication* (1972), 22: 353–374.

————, Sorenson, E., and Friesen, W. "Pan-cultural elements in facial displays of emotion." *Science* (1969), 164: 86–88.

Erikson, E. *Childhood and Society.* New York: W. W. Norton, 1963.

Ervin-Tripp, S., and Rosenthal, J. Unpublished data, 1968.

Fernald, G. *Remedial Techniques in Basic School Subjects.* New York: McGraw-Hill Book Co., 1943.

Flavell, J. *The Developmental Psychology of Jean Piaget.* New York: D. Van Nostrand Co., 1963.

Fleming, J. Introduction. In *Psycholinguistics and the Teaching of Reading,* edited by S. Goodman and J. Fleming. Newark, Del.: International Reading Association, 1969.

————. "The state of the apes." *Psychology Today* (1974), 7: 31–46.

Fodor, J., and Bever, T. "The psychological reality of linguistic segments." *Journal of Verbal Learning & Verbal Behavior,* (1965), 4: 414–420.

Fouts, R. "Acquisition and testing of gestural signs in four young chimpanzees." *Science* (1973), 180: 978–980.

Frank, J., and Levinson, H. "Dysmetric dyslexia and dyspraxia: Hypothesis and study." *Journal of the American Academy of Child Psychiatry* (1973), 12: 690–701.

Freeman, R. "Controversy over patterning as a treatment for brain damage in children." *Journal of the American Medical Association* (1967), 202: 385–388.

Freud, S. *The Basic Writings of Sigmund Freud*, edited by A Brill. New York: The Modern Library, 1938.

_____. *The Psychopathology of Everyday Life*. New York: Mentor Books, 1951.

Fry, D. "The development of the phonological system in the normal and deaf child." In *The Genesis of Language*, edited by F. Smith and G. Miller. Cambridge, Mass.: The MIT Press, 1966.

Galin, D. Personal communication, 1975.

_____, and Ellis, R. "Asymmetry in evoked potentials as an index of lateralized cognitive processes: Relation to EEG alpha asymmetry." *Neuropsychologia* (1975), 13: 45–50.

Galin, D., and Ornstein, R. "Lateral specialization of cognitive mode." *Psychophysiology* (1972), 9: 412–418.

_____. "Hemispheric specialization and the duality of consciousness." In *Human Behavior and Brain Function*, edited by H. Wildroe. Springfield, Ill.: Charles C Thomas, 1973.

Gardner, R., and Gardner, B. "Teaching sign language to a chimpanzee." *Science* (1969), 165: 644–672.

Geschwind, N. "The anatomy of acquired disorders in reading." In *Reading Disability*, edited by J. Money. Baltimore: The Johns Hopkins Press, 1962.

_____. "Disconnection syndromes in animals and man." *Brain* (1965), 88: 237–294; 585–644.

_____. "Aphasia." *New England Journal of Medicine* (1971), 284: 654–656.

_____, and Levitsky, W. "Human brain: Left-right asymmetries in temporal speech region." *Science* (1968), 161: 186–187.

Gesell, A. "The ontogenesis of infant behavior." In *Manual of Child Psychology*, edited by L. Carmichael. New York: John Wiley & Sons, 1966.

Gibson, E. "Learning to read." *Science* (1965), 148: 1066–1072.

Gleason, H. *An Introduction to Descriptive Linguistics.* New York: Holt, Rinehart & Winston, 1961.

Gofman, H. "The physician's role in early diagnosis and management of learning disabilities." In *Learning Disabilities. Introduction to Educational and Medical Management,* edited by L. Tarnopol. Springfield, Ill.: Charles C Thomas, 1969.

Goldberg, H. "Vision, perception, and related facts in dyslexia." In *Dyslexia,* edited by A. Keeney and V. Keeney. St. Louis: The C. V. Mosby Co., 1968.

Goldstein, K. *After-effects of Brain-injury in War.* New York: Grune & Stratton, 1942.

Gore, A. "Just words." *Journal of the American Medical Association* (1965), 192: 113.

Graf, R. "Speed reading: Remember the tortoise." *Psychology Today* (1973), 7: 112–113.

Greenberg, J. "Some universals of grammar with particular reference to the order of meaningful elements." In *Universals of Language,* edited by J. Greenberg. Cambridge, Mass.: The MIT Press, 1963.

Griffin, D., Walton, H., and Ives, U. "Saccades as related to reading disorders." *Journal of Learning Disabilities* (1974), 7: 310–316.

Hallgren, B. "Specific dyslexia." *Acta Psychiatria et Neurologica* (1950), Supplement No. 65: 1–287.

Hanley, J. Personal communication, 1975.

Harlow, H., and Harlow, M. "Social deprivation in monkeys." *Scientific American* (1962), 20: 136–146.

Hécaen, H. "Brain mechanisms suggested by studies of parietal lobes." In *Brain Mechanisms Underlying Speech and Language,* edited by C. Millikan and F. Darley. New York: Grune & Stratton, 1967.

Hockett, C. *A Course in Modern Linguistics.* New York: Crowell, Collier & Macmillan, 1958.

_____. "The origins of speech." *Scientific American* (1966), 203: 89–96.

Holm, V., and Kunze, L. "Effect of chronic otitis media on language and speech development." *Pediatrics* (1969) 43: 833–839.

Hymes, D. "The anthropology of communication." In *Human Communication Theory*, edited by F. Dance. New York: Holt, Rinehart & Winston, 1967.

Ingvar, D., and Schwartz, M. "Blood flow patterns induced in the dominant hemisphere by speech and reading." *Brain* (1974), 97: 273–288.

Jakobson, R., and Halle, M. *Fundamentals of Language*. The Hague: Mouton, 1956.

Johnson, D., and Myklebust, H. *Learning Disabilities: Educational Principles and Practices*. New York: Grune & Stratton, 1967.

Kawi, A., and Pasamanick, B. "Association of factors of pregnancy with reading disorders." *Journal of the American Medical Association* (1958), 166: 1420–1423.

Kinsbourne, M. "School problems." *Pediatrics* (1973), 52: 697–710.

————, and Warrington, E. "Developmental factors in reading and writing backwardness." In *The Disabled Reader: Education of the Dyslexic Child*, edited by J. Money. Baltimore: Johns Hopkins Press, 1966.

Klasen, E. *The Syndrome of Specific Dyslexia*. Baltimore: University Park Press, 1972.

Knobloch, H., and Pasamanick, B. "Syndromes of minimal cerebral damage." *Journal of the American Medical Association* (1959), 170: 1384–1387.

Kolers, P. "Three stages of reading." In *Psycholinguistics and Reading*, edited by F. Smith. New York: Holt, Rinehart, & Winston, 1973.

La Du, B. "Histidinemia." In *The Metabolic Bases of Inherited Disease*, edited by J. Stanbury, J. Wingaarden, and D. Fredrickson. New York: McGraw-Hill Book Co., 1972.

Laird, C. *The Miracle of Language.* Greenwich, Conn.: Fawcett Publications, 1953.

Lamb, S. "The Illinois Test of Psycholinguistic Abilities." In *Learning Disabilities: Introduction to Educational and Medical Management,* edited by L. Tarnopol. Springfield, Ill.: Charles C Thomas, 1969.

Langer, J. "Disequilibrium as a source of development." In *Trends and Issues in Developmental Psychology,* edited by P. Mussen, J. Langer, and M. Covington. New York: Holt, Rinehart, & Winston, 1969a.

————. *Theories of Development.* New York: Holt, Rinehart, & Winston, 1969b.

Lee, L. "Developmental sentence type; a method for comparing normal and deviant syntactic development." *Journal of Speech and Hearing Disorders* (1966), 31: 311–330.

————. Personal communication, 1967.

Lenneberg, E. "Language disorders in childhood." *Harvard Educational Review* (1964), 34: 152–177.

————. *The Biological Foundations of Language.* New York: John Wiley & Sons, 1967.

Levy, H., Shih, V., and Madigan, P. "Routine newborn screening for histidinemia." *New England Journal of Medicine* (1974), 291: 1214–1219.

Lewis, V., Ehrhardt, A., and Money, J. "Genital operations in girls with the adrenogenital syndrome." *Obstetrics and Gynecology* (1970), 36: 11–15.

Luria, A. *The Working Brain.* New York: Basic Books, 1973.

MacNeilage, P., Rootes, T., and Chase, R. "Speech production and perception in a patient with severe impairment of somesthetic perception and motor control." *Journal of Speech & Hearing Research* (1967), 10: 449–467.

Makita, K. "The rarity of reading disability in Japanese

children." *American Journal of Orthopsychiatry* (1968), 38: 599–614.

McGlone, J., and Kertesz, A. "Sex differences in cerebral processing of visuospatial tasks." *Cortex* (1973), 9: 313–320.

McNeil, M., and Hamre, C. "A review of measures of lateralized cerebral hemispheric functions." *Journal of Learning Disabilities* (1974), 7: 375–383.

McNeill, D. "The creation of language by children." In *Psycholinguistic Papers: Proceedings of the 1966 Edinburgh Conference,* edited by J. Lyons and R. J. Wales. Edinburgh: Edinburgh University Press, 1966a.

————. "Developmental psycholinguistics." In *The Genesis of Language,* edited by F. Smith and G. Miller. Cambridge, Mass.: The MIT Press, 1966b.

Menyuk, P. "Comparison of grammar of children with functionally deviant and normal speech." *Journal of Speech and Hearing Research* (1964), 7: 109–121.

Meredith, W., Watson, M., Bachman, R., Richmon, J., and Rosenthal, J. Unpublished data, 1975.

Miller, G. *Language and Communication.* New York: McGraw-Hill Book Co., 1951.

Miller, W., and Ervin, S. "The development of grammar in child language." In *The Acquisition of Language,* edited by U. Bellugi and R. Brown. Monographs of the Society for Research in Child Development (1964), 29(1): 9–33.

Money, J. "Dyslexia: A postconference review." In *Reading Disability,* edited by J. Money. Baltimore: The Johns Hopkins Press, 1962.

————, Alexander, D., and Ehrhardt, A. "Visuo-constructional deficit in Turner's syndrome." *Journal of Pediatrics* (1966), 69: 126–127.

Mowrer, O. "On the psychology of talking birds." In *Learning Theory and Personality Dynamics.* New York: Ronald, 1950.

Napier, J. "The evolution of the hand," *Scientific American* (1962), 207: 56–62.

Neill, A. *Summerhill.* New York: Hart Publishing Co., 1960.

Neimark, E. "An information-processing approach to cognitive development." *Transactions of the New York Academy of Sciences* (1971), 33: 516–528.

Neisser, V. *Cognitive Psychology.* New York: Appleton-Century-Crofts, 1966.

Nicholls, J. "Responsibilities of the ophthalmologist." In *Dyslexia,* edited by A. Keeney and V. Keeney. St. Louis: The C. V. Mosby Co., 1968.

Ogg, O. *The 26 Letters.* New York: Thomas Y. Crowell Co., 1948.

Ornstein, R. *The Psychology of Consciousness.* San Francisco: W. H. Freeman & Co., 1972.

Orton, S. "Word-blindness in school children." *Archives of Neurology and Psychiatry* (1925), 14: 581–615.

————. *Reading, Writing, and Speech Problems in Children.* New York: W. W. Norton Co., 1937.

Pearson, G. "A survey of learning difficulties in children." In *The Psychoanalytic Study of the Child.* New York: International Universities Press, 1952.

Penfield, W., and Rasmussen, T. *The Cerebral Cortex of Man.* New York: Macmillan, 1950.

Penfield, W., and Roberts, L. *Speech and Brain Mechanisms.* Princeton, N.J.: Princeton University Press, 1959.

Piaget, J. *Psychology of Intelligence.* Paterson, N.J.: Littlefield, Adams & Co., 1963.

Prechtl, H. "Reading difficulties as a neurological problem in childhood." In *Reading Disability,* edited by J. Money. Baltimore: The Johns Hopkins Press, 1962.

Rabinovitch, R. "Reading and learning disabilities." In *American Handbook of Psychiatry,* edited by S. Arieti. New York: Basic Books, 1959.

―――――. "Reading problems in children: Definitions and classifications." In *Dyslexia*, edited by A. Keeney and V. Keeney. St. Louis: The C. V. Mosby Co., 1968.

Rapaport, D. "The structure of psychoanalytic theory." In *Psychology: A Study of a Science*. Vol. 3, *Formulations of the Person and the Social Context*, edited by S. Koch. New York: McGraw-Hill Book Co., 1959.

Rawson, M. *Developmental Language Disability*. Baltimore: The Johns Hopkins Press, 1968.

Robbins, M. "A study of the validity of Delacato's theory of neurological organization." *Exceptional Children* (1966), 32: 517–523.

―――――. "Test of the Doman-Delacato rationale with retarded readers." *Journal of the American Medical Association* (1967), 202: 389–393.

Rosenthal, J. "Pseudo-pseudo-hypoparathyroidism in identical female twins." *Proceedings of the Second International Congress of Human Genetics*, Rome (1961), 1: 294–296.

―――――. "A preliminary psycholinguistic study of children with learning disabilities." *Journal of Learning Disabilities* (1970), 3: 11–15.

―――――. *Hazy? Crazy? and/or Lazy? The Maligning of Children with Learning Disabilities*. San Rafael, Calif.: Academic Therapy Publications, 1973a.

―――――. "Selfesteem in dyslexic children." *Academic Therapy* (1973b), 9: 27–39.

Rosenthal, R., and Jacobson, L. *Pygmalion in the Classroom: Teacher Expectation and Pupils' Intellectual Development*. New York: Holt, Rinehart, & Winston, 1968.

Ruddell, R. "Psycholinguistic implications for a systems of communication model." In *Psycholinguistics and the Teaching of Reading*, edited by K. Goodman and J. Fleming. Newark, Del.: International Reading Association, 1969.

Sachs, J. "Recognition memory for syntactic and semantic aspects of connected discourse." *Perception & Psycholinguistics* (1967), 2: 437–442.

Sapir, E. *Language.* New York: Harcourt, Brace, & World, 1921.

Sasanuma, S. "Kanji versus Kana processing in alexia with transient agraphia: a case report." *Cortex* (1974), 10: 89–97.

Satterfield, J., Lesser, L., and Cantwell, D. "EEG aspects of the diagnosis and treatment of minimal brain dysfunction." In *Minimal Brain Dysfunction,* edited by F. de la Cruz, B. Fox, and R. Roberts. New York: New York Academy of Sciences, 1973.

Saunders, R. "Dyslexia: Its phenomenology." In *Reading Disability,* edited by J. Money. Baltimore: The Johns Hopkins Press, 1962.

Savin, H., and Perchonock, E. "Grammatical structure and the immediate recall of English sentences." *Journal of Verbal Learning & Verbal Behavior* (1965), 4: 348–353.

Scheflen, A. "The significance of posture in communication systems." *Psychiatry* (1964), 27: 316–331.

Scott, J. "Critical periods in behavioral development." *Science* (1962), 138: 949–958.

Seiderman, A. "A look at perceptual-motor training." *Academic Therapy* (1972), 7: 315–321.

Shuy, R. "Some language and cultural differences in a theory of reading." In *Psycholinguistics and the Teaching of Reading,* edited by S. Goodman and J. Fleming. Newark, Del.: International Reading Association, 1969.

Sklar, B. "A computer classification of normal and dyslexic children using spectral estimates of their EEGs." Unpublished doctoral dissertation, University of California Los Angeles, 1971.

Sloan, R. "Neuronal histogenesis, maturation, and organization related to speech development." *Journal of Communication Disorders* (1967), 1: 1–15.

Slobin, D. "Comments on developmental psycholinguistics." In *The Genesis of Language*, edited by F. Smith and G. Miller. Cambridge, Mass.: The MIT Press, 1966.

————. Personal communication, 1967.

————. *Psycholinguistics*. Glenview, Ill.: Scott, Foresman, 1971.

Spitz, R. "Hospitalism." In *Psychoanalytic Study of the Child*, Vol. 1. New York: International Universities Press, 1945.

Strauss, A., and Kephart, N. *Psychopathology and Education of the Brain Injured Child. Progress in Clinic and Theory*. New York: Grune & Stratton, 1955.

Strauss, A., and Lehtinen, L. *Psychopathology and Education of the Brain-injured Child*. New York: Grune & Stratton, 1947.

Subirana, A. "The problem of cerebral dominance. The relationship between handedness and language function." *Bulletin of the Orton Society* (1964), 14: 45–68.

Swanson, W. "Optometric vision therapy—How successful is it in the treatment of learning disorders?" *Journal of Learning Disabilities* (1972), 5: 285–290.

Ullmann, S. "Semantic universals." In *Universals of Language*, edited by J. Greenberg. Cambridge, Mass.: The MIT Press, 1963.

Von Frisch, K. *Bees: Their Vision, Chemical Senses, and Language*. Ithaca, N.Y.: Cornell University Press, 1950.

Wardhaugh, R. "The teaching of phonics and comprehension: a linguistic evaluation." In *Psycholinguistics and the Teaching of Reading*, edited by K. Goodman and J. Fleming. Newark, Del.: International Reading Association, 1969.

Washburn, S. "Tools and human evolution." *Scientific American* (1960), 203: 63–75.

Webster's Seventh New Collegiate Dictionary. Springfield, Mass.: G. & C. Merriam Co., 1971.

Weikart, D., Rogers, L., Adcock, C., and McClelland, D. *The Cognitively Oriented Curriculum.* Urbana, Ill.: University of Illinois, 1971.

Werner, H. *Comparative Psychology of Mental Development.* New York: International Universities Press, 1948.

_____. "The concept of development from a comparative and organismic point of view." In *The Concept of Development,* edited by D. Harris. Minneapolis, Minn.: University of Minnesota Press, 1957.

White, L. "The Symbol." In *The Science of Culture.* New York: Farrar, Straus, & Cudahy, 1949.

Witelson, S., and Pallie, W. "Left hemisphere specialization for language in the new born." *Brain* (1973), 96: 641–646.

Wolman, I. "Some prominent developments in childhood nutrition: 1972." *Clinical Pediatrics* (1973), 12. 72–82.

Woods, E. *What Is Reading Dynamics?* Westport, Conn.: Diversified Educational Publishing Corp., 1969.

Woolsey, C., and Settlage, P. "Patterns of localization in the precentral motor cortex of Macaca mulatta." *Federation Proceedings of the American Society for Experimental Biology* (1950), 9: 140. Cited by Ruch, T. "Motor systems." In *Handbook of Experimental Psychology,* edited by S. Stevens. New York: John Wiley & Sons, 1951.

Yen, W., and Meredith, W. Personal communication, 1974.

Index

About the Author

Joseph H. Rosenthal, M.D., is director of the Learning Disabilities Clinic of the Department of Pediatrics at the Kaiser-Permanente Medical center in Oakland, California. He is also an assistant clinical professor in the Department of Psychiatry at the University of California Medical School at San Francisco. Dr. Rosenthal earned his B.A. degree from New York University and his M.D. degree from the Downstate Medical Center in Brooklyn, New York. He also received his M.A. in psychology at the University of California, Berkeley and is currently working toward his Ph.D. in physiologic psychology at the University of California, San Francisco.

Dr. Rosenthal is the author of *Hazy . . . ? Crazy . . . ? and/or Lazy . . . ? The Maligning of Children with Learning Disabilities*. In addition, he has written and lectured widely on the subject of learning disabilities. Dr. Rosenthal has served as consultant to several school districts and universities. He has also served the State of California and the California Association for Neurologically Handicapped Children in connection with learning disabilities.